The
Millennium
Bug
Debugged

HANK HANEGRAAFF

The Millennium Bug Debugged

BETHANY HOUSE PUBLISHERS
MINNEAPOLIS, MINNESOTA 55438

Published by Bethany House Publishers
A Ministry of Bethany Fellowship International
11400 Hampshire Avenue South
Minneapolis, Minnesota 55438
www.bethanyhouse.com

Printed in the United States of America by
Bethany Press International, Minneapolis, Minnesota 55438

Library of Congress Cataloging-in-Publication Data

Hanegraaff, Hank.
    The millennium bug debugged: the story behind all the Y2K sensationalism / by Hank Hanegraaff.
       p.   cm.
    Includes bibliographical references and index.
    ISBN 0–7642–2339–9 (pbk.)
    1. Year 2000 date conversion (Computer systems)—Religious aspects—Christianity. I. Title.
BR115.Y43H36   1999   99–6769
270.8'28—dc21   CIP

To Paul Young

a friend and faithful follower of Christ
whose "soul thirsts for God."

Acknowledgments

First, I would like to express appreciation to Carol Johnson and the staff of Bethany House Publishers. Not only are they a pleasure to work with but their courage and commitment to publishing a book that presents the other side of the story is refreshing.

Furthermore, I would also like to acknowledge the board and staff of the Christian Research Institute for their encouragement and support. I am especially grateful to Sam Wall and the research staff for continuously updating me on the latest developments regarding Y2K; to Elliott Miller, editor-in-chief of the *Christian Research Journal*, for encouraging me to pursue this project; to Stephen Ross, special assistant to the president, for his editorial input and ferocious commitment to detail; and to Bob Hunter for collation of the bibliography and subject index.

Finally, I am deeply grateful to Kathy and the kids—Michelle, Katie, David, John Mark, Hank, Jr., Christina, Paul Steven, and Faith. They are not only the spice of life but my greatest earthly treasure.

Above all, I am supremely thankful for the indwelling power of God, through Whom I live and move and have my being. To Him be the glory!

Contents

5) How will personal items such as curling irons and
   clock radios be affected by Y2K?
6) Will ATMs be ready for the new millennium?
7) Will banks be ready for the new millennium?

Before You Begin

If ever there was an issue I did not want to tackle, it was Y2K! Frankly, I did everything I could to avoid it. But as major broadcast ministries ranging from *Focus on the Family* to the *Old Time Gospel Hour* publicly aired their perspectives on the "millennium bug," calls and communications from virtually every sector of society cascaded into the offices of the Christian Research Institute. Pastors were desperate to know what to communicate to their congregations. Parishioners wanted to know whether they should pull their savings out of the bank or retirement accounts. One couple wondered whether they should bring a baby into a world about to go berserk. The sentiments ranged from acrimony to anxiety. Here are just a few examples:

> Hank,
>   I am extremely disappointed in your comments regarding the year 2000 computer problem. It would appear that your problem is as much political as it is spiritual. This is very unfortunate. The liberal nature of your opinions and your vile disregard for others' opinions indicates to me that you need to examine your position. I am guessing that

you fit into the camp of liberal ministers who spew liberal left wing "tolerance."

If I had to guess, I am guessing that you voted for our sitting criminal president both times, and will probably vote for his earth worshipping predecessor [*sic*].

I do not know what the year 2000 computer problem will bring. I have done consulting work and enormous research regarding the problem ... my counsel regarding Y2K is completely Biblical. I always tell people that they should be prepared for a month without lights, water, electricity or income. . . .

Most of the individuals that you attempt to discredit on your show attempt to tell people that they are not trying to create panic, but rather pass on information that could be useful. If you have taken the time to research the problem you know that. If you know that, you stand to hold the blood of many people on your hands. . . . I personally feel you should spend as little time as possible discussing the year 2000 problem. You are only discrediting yourself among the thinking listeners that you have and you are potentially hurting those that follow you.[1]

Dear Hank:

My husband recently listened to a broadcast of Dr. Dobson, his guest was Michael Hyatt who has a Y2K book out. My husband really took to heart the ideas, insights expressed by Mr. Hyatt and gave them more credence because of Dr. Dobson. Although I understand that Y2K is of concern, I felt comfortable that the Lord will provide, will take care of his church. However, Mr. Hyatt suggested doing things like storing water, buying extra canned goods, candles, as though the way of life we know now will end in eleven months. I'm curious to know your thoughts on Y2K and have hesitated buying Mr. Hyatt's book because it seems so extreme. My husband and I were planning to buy a home soon and he has decided we should wait 'til after the new year because this was suggested by Mr. Hyatt. I suddenly began thinking that I have taken all this too lightly and need to begin preparing. I look forward to your response and guidance in this matter.[2]

Dear CRI,

Greetings from the Mexican churches (some) here in South Texas. There is a *Panic* among the Christian brethren because of the Y2K problem. A well known Hispanic minister (Doctor in Theology) came to San Antonio, Texas and said the following:

1. The year 2000 is significant.
2. *One second* after midnight, December 31, 1999, I *do not* want to be in a plane, or an elevator, or hooked up to life support systems in a hospital, because *for sure* they are going to fail!
3. So he urged us to buy land out of the city, plant gardens, store food and water, and learn how to live off the land without having to go to the city; for computers will fail and we'll be out of jobs, out of banking, out of electricity, we won't be able to shop at the grocery store!

Honestly, you do not know how much hysteria this has caused; some people are going *"nuts"*!!! *Please, please, please* send me . . . information on *Y2K* and what to do!

I've written other ministries asking for information about this, but to *no* avail, no one answers me, I hope you do.[3]

One letter above all others caught my attention. It was written by a technology-savvy listener who stated that he had done "significant computer work in banking, biomedical systems, accounting systems, electric utilities, computer operating systems, and many other areas relevant to Y2K." He had also "designed and developed the hardware and software of computers from the chip level up." His concern was that Y2K was being overblown by Christian broadcasters.

He warned Christian leaders that more harm would likely result from frightening people than would result from the problem itself. "When people are brought to panic," he wrote, "great harm can be done. They may make irrational decisions and endanger their own health and financial condition as well as that of others." This letter, addressed not only to me but to other Christian broadcasters including Dr. James Dobson, offered succinct reasons why Y2K would not likely "become a super disaster":

> The premise for thinking that computers are going to fail and cause the failure of other systems goes like this: Everybody has seen computer output that shows dates as two digits. People go on to erroneously assume additional facts:
>
> FAULTY PREMISE 1: Most computer programs use dates in a significant way.
>
> FAULTY PREMISE 2: Seeing dates expressed as two digits implies that a program will not be able to calculate properly in the year 2000.
>
> FAULTY PREMISE 3: There are many important computer programs that will mis-control important . . . [information in ways that] people will be largely helpless to prevent. . . .
>
> Every computer program or subprogram can be put into one of the following categories:
>
> Category 1: The program doesn't use dates or the passage of time at all.

Category 2: The program only uses dates and time to "label" things (as you might put a date with your signature on a document).

Category 3: The program uses time, but only in a "relative" way. It is concerned with how much time has elapsed, but it is not concerned with the date, except possibly as in category 2 above.

Category 4: The program keeps track of dates and does do calculations that depend on the distance between two dates.[4]

The writer of this letter used the categories above to present the case that Y2K will not be as significant a problem as some would have us believe. He then presented ministry leaders with a challenge:

ONE WAY TO JUDGE THE PROBLEM FOR YOURSELF

If you feel that the technical computer problems of Y2K are worthy of alarming people, perhaps you are able to invest a little of your own organization's resources to make a small individual assessment. (I know most of you really struggle with resources. However, I'd suggest that using some of your resources to gain some firsthand authority about the problem might be better stewardship than causing listeners unnecessary harm by panic. I know you would never intentionally harm your listeners in this way.)

To do this experiment, you need to borrow or lease some computers similar to those used in your organization and borrow or hire some people to help run them.

Duplicate your own computer operations on the borrowed systems, but set the date on these systems to the corresponding day of the month in December 1999. Then each day, do all of your usual computer processing on both your original system and on the borrowed systems (moving the dates entered on the borrowed system ahead by an appropriate amount).

At the end of the month, your borrowed system will go through Y2K. See what problems result from this for the next few days to several weeks. Keep in mind that you probably did nothing to prepare your computer applications for Y2K. In many cases, it is unlikely that you will find any problems at all. If you have problems, it is unlikely that they are such that would bring your organization to a halt.

A similar approach was used with the computers on the Wall Street stock exchanges a few months ago, and they concluded that they would not have Y2K problems.[5]

In addition to letters from listeners, a never ending stream of literature from manuscripts to magazines daily flood into my office, many painting an unflattering picture of Christian leaders. The cover of *Time*'s January 18, 1999 issue featured a caricature of Christ with a sandwich board hanging over his shoulders that read, "THE END OF THE WORLD!?! Y2K insanity! Apocalypse Now! Will computers melt down? Will Society? A guide to MILLENNIUM MADNESS."

The article goes on to say that "most early 'roosters'—people who see apocalypse on the millennial horizon—came to their conclusions through a prism of religious belief."[6] The article profiles Calvinistic Reconstructionist Gary North who heads his own institute for Christian economics:

"Scary Gary's" website is by far one of the most popular Y2K panic centers. "In all of man's history," he has warned, "we have never been able to predict with such accuracy a worldwide disaster of this magnitude. The millennium clock keeps ticking. There is nothing we can do." But he has a few recommendations anyhow: buy gold and grain; quit your job; and find a remote cabin safe from the rioting hordes. He also recommends a two-year subscription (price: $225) to his newsletter, *Remnant Review*, an offer that appears to reflect a faith that, if nothing else, the mail will keep operating through 2000. As a subscriber incentive he promises "my report on 15 stocks which stand to benefit from this crisis."[7]

The article suggests that North actually hopes that America will collapse. He believes "it's part of his duty to bring it down, to be replaced by a Bible-based Reconstructionist state that will impose the death penalty on blasphemers, heretics, adulterers, gay men and women who have had abortions or sex before marriage."[8] The authors observe that there is a fine line between North's "warning against a calamity" and his motivation "for encouraging a panic."[9]

Christian leader Tim LaHaye is referred to as offering "maximalist warnings about Y2K" as well:

It "very well could trigger a financial meltdown," he [LaHaye] warned recently in an online-chat event, "leading to an international depression which would make it possible for the Antichrist or his emissaries to establish a one-world currency or a one-world economic system which will dominate the world commercially until it is destroyed."[10]

Likewise, Jerry Falwell is ridiculed for offering "vaunted biblical allegories to the Y2K crisis even as he cashes in: he's hawking a $25 video on Y2K that only half-jokingly suggests stockpiling ammo."[11]

Time notes that history "is littered with premature prophets of doom." The authors point to the Millerites as a prime example:

> One of America's largest millennial movements was led by William Miller, a 19th century farmer. On Oct. 22, 1844, many of his 50,000 followers took to the hilltops, waiting in vain for the appearance of Christ and an army of angels.[12]

Like *Time, Esquire* magazine used Y2K to satirize Christianity as a pathetic subculture desperately seeking validation. Although painful, the January 1999 issue of *Esquire* gives us a glimpse of the world's perspective on Christian leadership:

> In his press conference, in his speech, and on his television show, he continually drops names, exotic locales—"I was talking with Senator So-and-so today"; "The other day, I had a call from Beijing at seven in the morning, and not long after that, I was on the phone to someone in Moscow"—as though to say, I might be a bare-knuckled millenarian, but I'm plugged in. It works, too: Around the Founders, people are always saying things like, "Well, Pat Robertson knows *everybody*" and "Well, Dr. Robertson ought to know—he's in touch with senators, congressmen, business tycoons." Either a paradox or just a flat-out con: a man who derives his force from telling his flock that he, as a Christian leader, gives them a place at the table from which they, as Christians, have been excluded. No wonder he's always laughing.
>
> Of course, he—along with his creation, the Founders Inn—just embodies the larger paradox at the heart of Christianity: its simultaneous status as mainstream religion and apocalyptic cult. It's a mainstream apocalyptic cult, hence the interest in Y2K, a mainstream apocalypse. A reliable apocalypse. It's gonna happen. The only ques-

tion is, how bad—or good—is it going to be? And that's what we're here at the Founders Inn to find out. The only problem: Nobody knows, not even Pat Robertson. And so, as he stands before us in his stellar white shirt, in his beautiful blue suit, he does what he usually does—uses that humorless hilarity, that awed conflation of grim assurance and chuckling alarm. "What we are looking at is a man-made global crisis of such magnitude that nobody really can assess it," he says. No, "this isn't like the collapse of the Roman Empire, and we don't have Vandals and the Goths and Visigoths ready to destroy our society," and yet . . . well, Pat is an absolute master at mining the subjunctive, at cultivating the seed of the threat buried inside each unrealized instance. "I believe the very real possibility exists. . . . This is a very, very real possibility. . . . It is entirely possible that . . . I don't know if anyone can verify that, but . . ." Oil refineries shutting down because of one uncooperative computer chip; foreign countries quarantined from the global telecommunications network because they haven't updated their computers; the resulting "economic chaos around the world"; supposed doomsayers coming to be "known as prophets in the period of the new millennium." He's a pretty scary guy, this Pat Robertson, not because he'll say what *will* happen, but because he'll never, ever say what *won't*. Indeed, so gleefully ambiguous is his presentation that by its conclusion, he has delivered what might seem an arcane technical problem into the realm of belief, so that what's going to happen matters far less than what we, as Christians, *want* to happen, and what we, as Christians, want to happen is this: for the church to seize the opportunity presented by dire circumstance and enjoy its "finest hour."[13]

The proliferation of such magazine articles along with an escalating stream of manuscripts and other materials produced ever-increasing pressure for me to respond. In addition, as I traveled around the world, pastors and parishioners alike seemed to be asking the exact same question, "What's going to happen to us as a result of Y2K?" Through letters, e-mails, voice-mails, *Bible Answer Man* broadcast calls, and other communications it became abundantly clear that I needed to launch a primary source research project.

I proceeded, fully aware that I would pay a significant personal price for speaking out against the selling and sensationalism surrounding this issue. Already I have been accused of "breeding complacency" within the body of Christ. Some even suggest I am endangering the lives of my wife and eight children. And as documented above, it has been asserted that "I stand to hold the blood of many people" on my hands.

It is my firm conviction, however, that the ministry is not a place to strive for popularity or political correctness. Rather, my concern must be for the well-being of the body of Christ. As evidenced by the letters above, people are being significantly frightened by what they are hearing from Christian leaders regarding Y2K. I am deeply grieved over the spiritual, emotional, and financial havoc that so many have already suffered.

It is my prayer that this material will (1) provide a much needed antidote; (2) provide Christians with discernment skills so the next time they face an issue like Y2K—as they surely will—they will be equipped to discern wheat from chaff and heat from light; and (3) produce a greater awareness of the damage done by selling fear, sloppy journalism, sophistry, "Scriptorture," and schisms in the church.

Because reckless rumors, spurious statistics, and anecdotal arguments regarding Y2K are proliferating at breakneck speed, it is virtually impossible to deal with every one of them. However, the principles encapsulated in *The Millennium Bug Debugged* will equip you to unmask such deceptions for yourself.[14]

As with other crucial issues that I have addressed over the last decade, my sentiments are best summarized by the words of Dr. Abraham Kuyper (1837–1920):

> When principles that run against your deepest convictions begin to win the day, then battle is your calling, and peace has become sin; you must, at the price of dearest peace, lay your convictions bare before friend and enemy, with all the fire of your faith.[15]

We begin our journey by carefully examining the perspectives of Christian leaders that I greatly admire, such as Dr. D. James Kennedy and Dr. James Dobson. Before we are through, however, I will also address the materials of known sensationalists such as Chuck Missler and Don McAlvany. In the following pages I not only provide their perspectives (along with those of a host of others) but a careful analysis of these perspectives in light of facts.

Chapter 1

Seven Christian Leaders and Their Y2K Perspectives

Dr. D. James Kennedy

It was one of those mornings you don't soon forget. I arrived in Miami in the wee hours of the morning. My luggage was not as fortunate. By the time I got to the hotel it was 3 A.M. Sunday morning. After several hours of restless sleep, I awoke with a start, looked at my watch, and immediately realized I was already too late.

I had intended to drive to Fort Lauderdale to worship at Coral Ridge Presbyterian Church. Instead, I turned on the television just in time to hear Dr. D. James Kennedy announce that his message was titled "Y2K AND YOU." Although disappointed that I would not be able to attend Coral Ridge in person, I was delighted with the theme of Kennedy's Sunday morning message.

Dr. Kennedy mounted his pulpit, looked at his congregation, and said, "Today I want to do one thing: I want to get your attention. I mean: *I really want to get your attention!* Let me say this: I will have your attention and if I don't have it, you are going to be woefully sorry. For your sake, your family's sake, the church's sake, the nation's sake, please give me your attention."[1]

Kennedy assured his flock that he had devoted significant attention to the subject of Y2K: "I want to say that in the last six months I have spent a great deal of time studying this problem through numerous books, tapes, thousands of pages of data. I couldn't begin to tell you one-tenth of what it is all about, but I want to give some idea."[2]

He then went on to paint a very unpleasant picture: "Let me say that though today you may see a very dark cloud coming, I assure you that that dark cloud is going to catch the unprepared and drench them like they have never been drenched. Some people will never even know until it hits them, and when it does, it will be very similar to walking into a spinning airplane propeller. They won't even know what happened."[3]

There was, however, a silver lining. As Kennedy put it, "Spiritually we are heading for the greatest opportunities perhaps in the history of the church because people will be open to hear the Gospel as they have never been before. As the great god of mammon collapses on his face, people will be looking for help."[4]

Kennedy explained that there would be other opportunities for those who did not succumb to denial: "There are great opportunities not only of witness, but actually even for your own gain. Some people will be wiped out. Some people will get rich. It all depends on whether or not you find out or you say, 'Wha' happened?' "[5]

When someone I admire as much as Dr. Kennedy devotes "a great deal of time" studying a problem, it would be foolhardy for me not to carefully consider his conclusions. Thus, I listened carefully to his three-part television series on Y2K.[6]

First, according to Kennedy, the scope of the Y2K dilemma is so enormous that for all practical purposes it is insurmountable. As Kennedy put it, one large government agency put 400 full-time programmers to work on Y2K in 1991 and in five years were only able to find and correct 20 percent of the noncompliant computer codes.[7] Kennedy expressed concern that despite the enormity of the problem the typical American remains cavalier. He used his wife, Anne, as an example. When he explained the Y2K problem to her, she responded, "Well, Bill Gates will fix it." Kennedy had to warn his wife that even Bill Gates admitted, "I can't fix it. It's bigger than I am."[8]

Furthermore, Kennedy provided concrete examples of how Y2K was already affecting society. He pointed out that "one 104-year-old woman in Minnesota, in anticipation of this [Y2K], received a letter from the government telling her it was time to enroll in kindergarten."[9] Not only that, according to Kennedy, "Already, some prisoners have been allowed to leave prisons because of the foreshadowings of this problem by computers."[10] In addition, he pointed out that banks may well face an enormous problem as well: "January 1 comes on Saturday in 2000, but in 1900, it was Tuesday, so all of the bank vaults may be open or closed when they should be the other way around."[11]

Finally, Kennedy made it clear that he is not alone in his alarm over what could happen as a result of Y2K. He quoted men like Michael Hyatt who say that "preparing for Y2K is very much like buying insurance," and recommended Hyatt's "excellent book, *The Millennium Bug: How to Survive the Coming Chaos*."[12] The cover of Hyatt's book provides further perspective on just how serious the Y2K crisis may be:

> When the clock strikes midnight on January 1, 2000, computer systems all over the world will begin spewing out bad data—or stop working altogether.
>
> The result is going to be a billion times worse than the worst computer crash you have ever experienced—or could imagine[13]. . . . The results will be catastrophic.[14]

In addition to Hyatt, Kennedy quoted Don McAlvany who said,

> If the power grid goes down—if the utility company just doesn't make it and doesn't become Y2K compliant—the following will be impacted: water, sewer; lights; heat; all electrical equipment; all transportation, including air transport, trains, trucking, buses, and subways; traffic lights; street lights; gas stations; food supplies and distribution; grocery stores; restaurants; refrigeration; law enforcement; telephones and all telecommunications—except for short wave and radio broadcasts from non-affected areas to portable battery-charged radios or short-wave receivers; all computers; the Internet; hospitals and most traditional medical care; the banks, including ATMs in a blacked-out area; and the stock market. *All of this would be taking place in the dead of winter.*[15]

Kennedy pointed out that someone had the temerity to warn him, "You are going to ruin your credibility." In keeping with his convictions, however, he responded, "Dear folks, I am a pastor and you are my flock. Which is more important: your well-being or my credibility?"[16] He went on to point out the stark contrast between himself and most preachers:

> Most preachers will never say anything to their people about [Y2K], and it's going to hit them mostly unprepared. But as a pastor, I am concerned for my flock. I am concerned for your souls, and I am concerned for your bodies and your well-being and your families as well.[17]

Kennedy insisted that his followers begin their preparation for the Y2K catastrophe as soon as possible.[18] He quoted Proverbs 22:3: "*A prudent man sees danger and takes refuge, but the simple keep going and suffer for it.*"[19] Kennedy advised listeners to start "stockpiling" immediately as follows:

> The prudent man would probably want to have water to drink for the next two or three months minimum . . . *you need to begin to stockpile basic foods* . . . you will need lamps and oil for your lamps, flashlights, and many batteries. . . . You want to be sure you have enough currency, whether in the form of dollars or silver or gold coins, so that you will be able to continue on for several months if you don't have availability to what money you have in the bank. . . . The great enemy after denial is procrastination. All of these things are going to get more expensive between now and 2000. . . . People are beginning to wake up, dear friends, and that awakening somewhere down the line is going to end up in panic.[20]

Dr. Jerry Falwell

Like Dr. D. James Kennedy, Dr. Jerry Falwell devoted three televised broadcasts to what he termed the "Y2K Computer Crisis."[21] He began his series with Proverbs 22:3 TLB, "A prudent man foresees the difficulties ahead and prepares for them; the simpleton goes blindly on and suffers the consequences."[22] Dr. Falwell assured his flock that he had "studied the problem carefully"[23] and that "Y2K has the potential to be a very big problem, worldwide in scope and without historical precedent."[24] Falwell said the problem cannot be fixed because "WE DO NOT HAVE ENOUGH PROGRAMMERS. . . . We have run out of programmers who could conceivably fix the problem."[25]

To underscore "how imprisoned we are to our own electronic systems," Falwell used a bank illustration: "If the computer recognizes January 1, 2000, which is a Saturday, as January 1, 1900, which was a Monday, the vault will swing open on Saturday and lock shut on Thursday."[26]

The number one myth, said Falwell, is that "someone will come up with a silver bullet at the last moment and solve the whole thing."[27] Like Kennedy, Falwell used his wife, Masel, as a prime example of how people fall prey to the myth that someone will come up with a silver bullet:

> My wife thinks it's going to be Bill Gates. She and I talked about this over recent times. She says, "Oh, honey, we've met Bill Gates. We know Bill Gates," she said, "and you know he is so bright, so brilliant, that he is going to come out at the last month and the last week"—of course, that's her wishful thinking, out of her scared mentality of this thing—that he's going to come forward and have the solution and, of course, make another $50 billion for himself in the process.[28]

Falwell warned that unless Gates finds the silver bullet to solve the Y2K crisis, his entire fortune might well be wiped out. Said Falwell, "We mentioned Bill Gates—$50 billion dollars. But most of that is in stock in an industry that we're talking about that may become worthless, unless Masel's prophecy comes true that he finds that silver bullet."[29]

Falwell personally sought out the official position of Gates' corporation and discovered that Y2K was "too big and overwhelming for even Microsoft."[30] While Falwell does not hold to the "silver bullet" mythology of his wife Masel, he does believe there is a silver lining to Y2K. Says Falwell,

> I believe that Y2K may be God's instrument to shake this nation, awaken this nation, and from this nation start revival that spreads the face of the earth before the rapture of the church. Now I don't want to stop you and tell you that the Lord is going to come in the year 2000, but I want to tell you I wouldn't be a bit surprised. I just some-

how feel that we are tiptoeing very close to the edge. . . . Things right now are completely out of control.[31]

To provide further perspective on the potential danger surrounding Y2K, Falwell twice repeated information from the cover of Michael Hyatt's *The Millennium Bug*:

In the early days of computers, programmers did not anticipate the problems and confusion that would accompany the new millennium. Older systems leave off the first two digits of the year so that computers will confuse the year 2000 with the year 1900. The results . . . will be catastrophic:

- Social Security checks will stop coming.
- Planes all over the world will be grounded.
- Credit card charges will be rejected.
- Military defense systems will fail.
- Police records and emergency communications will be inaccessible.
- There will be massive long-term power failures.
- Bank funds will be inaccessible.
- Insurance policies will appear to have expired.
- Telephone systems will fail to operate.
- IRS tax records and government funds will be unavailable.
- The Federal Reserve will be unable to clear checks.
- Timed security vaults will fail to open or close on time.
- Traffic signals will fail to function.
- Office systems will fail and your employer may go out of business.[32]

The cover copy of Hyatt's book goes on to say,

Already we have seen warning signs:
(1) An electric utility ran a series of tests on the city power

grid to see what would happen on January 1, 2000. The power system simply stopped working.

(2) Some credit cards with expiration dates three years hence had to be recalled—the machines reading them thought they had expired.

(3) Computers have already mistakenly ordered the destruction of tons of corned beef, believing they were more than 100 years old.

(4) A state prison computer misread the release date of prisoners and freed them prematurely.

(5) A 104-year-old woman was given a notice to enter kindergarten.[33]

In light of the concerns posed by Y2K, Falwell recommended that his followers begin "stockpiling" and warned that "procrastination might be our worst enemy." Said Falwell,

> We may be thinking about stockpiling nonperishable foods and common household goods. . . . We might be thinking and praying about developing alternative sources of heat and energy, and preparing an emergency medical kit and determining how to dispose of waste, how to secure an alternative form of currency. Remember, cash or credit may be worthless if the computers go down and no one can get to it. And stockpiling things like paper towels, toilet paper, and personal products, toothpaste, soap, matches or lighters, candles, kerosene lamps, coffee/tea (by all means), sugar, and, being from Campbell County, some ammunition, because if I'm blessed with a little food and my family is inside the house with me, I've got to be sure that I can persuade others not to mess with us.[34]

Dr. James Dobson

Dr. James Dobson describes Y2K as "a simple little problem that has enormous implications. The only question now is whether it will cause a brownout, a blackout, or a meltdown."[35] He devoted three radio broadcasts to the issue[36] and also aired an all-staff chapel meeting featuring Michael Hyatt.[37] At the conclusion of Hyatt's address, Dr. Dobson turned to face a stunned staff:

> Thank you, Mike. I think everybody is a little stunned, but if that's what is about to happen in any of the three scenarios, then we need to know it. I said on the air, and I hope you heard it, when we talked about this before, that our board member, Don Hodel, advised me to go ahead and share this kind of information with people, because that gives you an opportunity to prepare, and panic occurs when you haven't had the opportunity to prepare.[38]

Dobson, who spent a year reading about and studying the year 2000 problem,[39] told staff members that there were eight possible scenarios that concerned him:

> The first is terrorist activity, and with our being a little off-balance, it would be a good time to go for that.
>
> Second is massive civil disobedience. People take advantage of an opportunity to loot and to express their hostility, and when you've got people hungry and you have children hungry, then you have people panicking and that can lead to massive civil disobedience.
>
> Third is a Saddam Hussein-type aggressor who would recognize that our military is not ready or what have you.
>
> Fourth is a world economic crisis where we are already kind of concerned about what's happening there.
>
> Five is that present political leaders would refuse to yield power. What if you have a situation where we've had our last election for awhile because the voter rolls are on computer. That raises a lot of questions.

Six is sun-spots that are due. Every eleven years the sun develops this tremendous energy that is thrown out into the solar system, and the last time it fried some of our communications systems, and they're expecting it again, when? November of 1999.

And then, finally, is God's judgment. And that one, obviously, overrides all the rest of them.[40]

Michael Hyatt provided emphasis to Dr. Dobson's final point: "We could talk all afternoon about each of those, but I think your last one is the most important, and that is that I think there is a convergence of all different kinds of things happening and when you look back through the Scripture you see that when God brings judgment, it's *always* according to natural disasters."[41]

Hyatt told the staff of Focus on the Family that they did not have to wait until the year 2000 to get a glimpse of the future—we can already see warning signs. Hyatt began with an example from his book: "In Britain, computers at Marks & Anderson company have already mistakenly ordered the destruction of tons of corned beef, believing they were more than 100 years old."[42]

Hyatt provided other stories as well. He pointed out that "there was a state prison computer in Pennsylvania that ordered the release of prisoners whose release dates were scheduled into the next century and they thought that they had already served and were overdue for release."[43] In addition, said Hyatt, "there was a 104-year-old woman in Kansas who received a notice to enter kindergarten."[44]

In light of what is to come, Hyatt quoted Proverbs 22:3, "A prudent man sees danger and takes refuge, but the simple keep going and suffer for it." He then asked his audience this question: "Are you prudent or are you simple?"[45]

In response to questions, Hyatt provided practical financial advice as well. Among his recommendations: "[Take] 30 days of cash out of the system"[46] and buy used instead of new and expensive sleeping bags—"probably if you're in your home and if you're huddled together and you've got sufficient clothing, you'll get through it."[47]

Because of the potential for economic chaos, Hyatt said he "would rent" rather than buy—"I think that we're going to see a stock market devaluation first. Then I think we're going to see real estate deflation second. And so I think that you might be in a better position after that happens to buy something for less money later. So I don't think, personally, it's a good time to buy."[48]

Like Kennedy and Falwell, Hyatt sees a silver lining in Y2K. In concluding his Focus on the Family address, he said, "I think this could be the church's finest hour. I think this could be an opportunity for evangelism and ministry that we haven't seen in 100 years."[49]

In addition to Michael Hyatt, Dr. Dobson called on Chuck Missler as an expert witness. Missler was introduced as "the founder and chairman of the board of Koinonia House—a ministry on the cutting edge of technology for spreading the gospel worldwide— Chuck has served on the board of Computer Communications Industry Association in [Washington] D. C. for fifteen years."[50] Like others, Missler communicated that Y2K is an extraordinary opportunity for witness. In his words, "It's the biggest opportunity for ministry in 1000 years."[51]

National Religious Broadcasters

During their 1999 convention held January 30 through February 2, the National Religious Broadcasters (NRB) presented a forum titled "Y2K: Facing the Challenge." Larry Burkett pointed out that there are an estimated 300 to 350 million embedded chips in America and that three percent of these chips were not going to be compliant. The problem, he said, is that we don't know which of the nine million chips aren't going to work.[52]

Burkett went on to say that in his opinion "the far more severe aspect of Y2K is the economic side of Y2K. I believe there is going to be an economic disaster." Burkett advised, "Have enough cash reserved to be able to ride out a storm that I believe is going to come economically." He paraphrased Proverbs 22:3: "A wise man looks ahead and perceives a problem and will attempt to avoid it; the fool proceeds without caution and will pay a penalty."[53]

Burkett added that a friend of his who is spending hundreds of millions of dollars of company money to prepare for Y2K told him that "the failure rate among small businesses in America will be upwards of 25% and that the failure rate among the biggest companies in the world may be as high as 15% as a direct result of Y2K." There was, however, a silver lining. Said Burkett, "The good news is the IRS as we know it won't exist probably after the year 2000. Lie as they might, they're not going to be compliant."[54]

Chuck Missler weighed in during the National Religious Broadcasters' forum as well. He introduced himself as a Bible teacher with a background "as a high technology executive" who is "regarded as one of the pioneers in the computer industry."[55] According to Missler, the most terrifying part of Y2K is the problem of chips. He said his numbers were a little different than Larry Burkett's. Instead of the 300 to 350 million embedded chips suggested by Burkett, Missler said, "The estimates that I hear are that there are about 50 billion of them in our society."[56]

Missler went on to say that he "trafficked" with members of Fortune 500 companies who in the boardroom privately were white-knuckled about embedded chips. In addition, said Missler, "I serve with the Council of [sic] National Policy. We traffic heavily in Washington. It may shock you to discover there are serious, responsible people in Washington that suspect there won't be elections in the year 2000."[57]

Another NRB speaker was Bob Allen. Allen, who was introduced as "a producer for eight years with Dr. D. James Kennedy,"[58] said that he had probably spent "more than 2000 hours" studying the year 2000 crisis and had come to the conclusion that there is "a much greater likelihood that my life will be disrupted by Y2K, perhaps in a serious way, than that my house will burn down, that my car will be in a wreck, or that I'll have a major medical problem."[59]

Allen said he did not want "to create fear." However, when "the pilots of the modern technological culture" are carrying parachutes, it should get your attention. He pointed to examples of extraordinary measures people have taken to prepare, which included storing up "a year's worth of food."[60]

Allen was also privy to insider information: "I had many insiders who had sent me documents, sometimes very explicitly saying 'you don't know where you got this, you cannot reveal who I am or who I work for.'" He passed off about one hundred and fifty pages of this insider information to a couple of electrical engineers. After evaluating the "diagrams and black boxes," one became "very concerned," and the other—a designer of electrical power plants—now "has 150 fifty-five-gallon water barrels on order."[61]

Allen made it clear that the concerned believers he knew were not "wild-eyed crazies" like those "profiled in *Time* magazine":

> I've got several specialists who work in the oil and gas industry who are working on some of the embedded systems problems. I've got three people in telecommunications, two of them in Fortune 100, one of them is a Y2K project head. I've got one who's a government security specialist in California, a Y2K project head for a Fortune 10 company, a CIO of a major medical concern, a computer specialist at a Fortune 500 pharmaceuticals company, a

programmer with twenty years of international experience designing systems, a CIO of a Fortune 250 consumers' goods company, and on and on.[62]

Steve Farrar

Steve Farrar, a nationally known speaker for Promise Keepers,[63] says he spent over one thousand hours researching Y2K.[64] He endorses Michael Hyatt's *The Millennium Bug* as "the best thing that's out there" and says that Y2K cannot be fixed in time. "There's not enough time left. . . . There aren't enough programmers in the world to get it fixed. See, that's why I see the fingerprints of God all over this thing. Only God could have come up with something like this."[65]

Grant Jeffrey

Grant Jeffrey, prophecy teacher and author of *The Millennium Meltdown*, says that when computers make the transition from the year 1999 to the year 2000, "many of these engines of modern society will begin to crash or malfunction, precipitating a global crisis, the scope of which we have not experienced since World War II."[66] "The stock market and the banking systems . . . will suffer challenges not experienced since the Great Depression."[67] Furthermore, Jeffrey says, "The banking runs and accompanying liquidity crisis that may unfold as one of the consequences of the Y2K problem will also provide a credible rationale for the abolition of paper currency and coins throughout the world."[68]

Jeffrey goes on to say that "it is fascinating to realize that the rise of a one-world government and the introduction of a numerical device beneath the skin of the right hand or forehead that would enable a person to 'buy or sell' was actually prophesied by the ancient prophet John in the book of Revelation almost two thousand years ago. It is one of the final signs that Jesus Christ is about to return to establish his millennial kingdom on earth."[69]

Jeffrey provides a number of foreshadowings of the Y2K problem:

> In Michigan, for example, a 104-year-old woman received a letter from the school board advising her that she must be prepared to start school the following year. The school district computer had correctly calculated that from her date of birth she should be starting school in 1900. . . .
>
> There have been other problems, however, that don't rise to the level of national security but still must be regarded as serious. A faulty computer program in Canada recently miscalculated the court dates of dozens of criminals who were inadvertently released long before they should have been. Fortunately, the prisoners were quickly apprehended. . . .
>
> Recently, a power plant in England had to be shut down, the result of a single chip failure in one of the generators. But the chip is so inaccessible it cannot be replaced, which means that the entire plant will have to be abandoned.[70]

Says Jeffrey, "The book of Proverbs provides a fundamental spiritual principle that we should all take to heart: 'A prudent man foreseeth the evil, and hideth himself; but the simple pass on, and are punished' (Prov. 27:12 KJV). This compelling advice applies to this [Y2K] situation, as well as to all other dangers. The Lord considered this proverb so important that it is repeated again in Proverbs 22:3."[71] Jeffrey claims that almost everyone who has studied the Y2K crisis "began their research in a state of denial. However, after a period of time, every serious researcher has come to the conclusion that we are facing the greatest challenge in our lives."[72]

Dr. R. C. Sproul

Noted theologian Dr. R. C. Sproul has weighed in on Y2K as well. According to Dr. Sproul, Y2K presents the "possibility of a catastrophe unprecedented in the world's history."[73] Said Sproul: "For several months like a nervous Floridian tracking hurricane coordinates, I have been reading everything I can get my hands on regarding the Y2K problem. . . . In wading through the literature on this matter, I have passed through a sequence of psychological states. The sequence has moved from awareness to concern to alarm to action."[74]

Sproul believes that we may "possibly" see "the meltdown of civilization with one billion fatalities—the end of the world as we know it."[75] In the April 1999 *Tabletalk*—the magazine of Sproul's Ligonier Ministries—there is an article entitled "The Great Collapse,"[76] which provides an imaginary view of how the Y2K crisis may work out. In this story, a grandfather describes to his grandson what civilization was like prior to the end of 1999. The story does not paint a pretty picture:

> Shoppers went wild at a grocery store, and hanged three clerks from a lamppost outside. . . . The federal government declare[d] martial law. . . . Food riots became so frequent that the newspapers stopped reporting them. . . . Christ's Church continued its work, a .357 Magnum in one hand and a Bible in the other. . . . Fires lit the night sky red. . . . You have heard about the Y2K martyrs, those who stayed to serve, and were killed by the very people they sought to save.

In the story, such dates as April, July, August, and September of 1999 are crucial. In April, several states enter the 2000 fiscal year. In spite of promises, the computers simply lock up. In July, more states experience breakdowns in police, administration, record keeping, welfare, and so forth as the result of computer shutdowns. In August, the global positioning system fails and the government declares martial law. September brings even more severe consequences as computers cannot deal with "9/9/99." In the end, civilization as we know it today ceases to exist as a result of Y2K.

Dr. Gary North

Calvinistic Reconstructionist Dr. Gary North says, "Once I understood what the Millennium Bug will do I decided to take a huge risk: to stake my reputation on a hard-to-believe prediction. I saw that if my prediction is correct, those who believe me and act in terms of my forecast will be in a position to lead in 2000 and beyond."[77] Among Dr. North's predictions are that "the Millennium Bug is going to take down every national Christian ministry"; "a famine will begin . . . pestilence will be there too. Public health systems will break down when water treatment and even delivery cease"; "no more court system"; and "no more public schools."[78] In short, North predicts the end of Western civilization as we know it.[79]

Like North, one leader after another confesses that they once were in denial but after countless hours of serious study they felt compelled to warn their congregations or constituencies of impending doom. While it's easy to dismiss apocalyptic warnings from people who have a track record of irresponsibility, it's quite another to dismiss the perspectives of credible Christian leaders like Dr. James Dobson and Dr. D. James Kennedy who have both contributed immeasurably to the health and growth of the evangelical Christian church.

Thus we face the question: How does one think critically about this very complex and highly emotional issue given that so many Christian leaders are sounding the apocalyptic alarm? In other words, how can everyone be wrong? The first answer to that question is found in a practice I describe as *Selling Fear*.

Chapter 2

Selling Fear

In 1999 I had dinner with a Christian publisher who did not view Y2K as a significant problem for the culture. Rather, he saw it as an opportunity for making a substantial profit for his company. As he half jokingly put it, "This is our year to sell fear."

Michael Hyatt

Perhaps no one has been more successful in selling fear than Michael Hyatt. In a short span of time he has risen from virtual obscurity to a household name in the Christian community.[1] While Hyatt openly acknowledges a tremendous debt to the work of Gary North,[2] he is reverently quoted by sensationalists ranging from Chuck Missler to Don McAlvany and his books are promoted by ministers and ministries ranging from Falwell to Focus on the Family. Steve Farrar, who represents himself as a nationally known speaker for Promise Keepers, says Hyatt's book, *The Millennium Bug*, is "the best thing that's out there."[3] Likewise, Dr. D. James Kennedy recommends it as an "excellent book."[4]

In reality, however, Hyatt has made a business out of selling fear. Even a cursory glance at the cover of *The Millennium Bug* bears eloquent testimony to this truth. In raised white letters is the subtitle "How to Survive the Coming Chaos." On the back cover, Hyatt states that the results of Y2K "will be catastrophic." In bold type are dogmatic declarations ranging from "Social security checks will stop coming" to "Bank funds will be inaccessible."

To solve the Y2K problem, Hyatt's website sells everything from food to a book on how to barter. Using high pressure sales tactics, Hyatt sells his wares. Under the caption *"We've Been Sold Out!"* he writes, "With a recklessness that could only be conceived by a Beltway Bureaucrat, *our government sold our food reserves to those Third World and Communist countries! Now we are down to literally only a 30-day supply!"*[5] Says Hyatt: *"PANIC BUYING may occur in late 1999 as year 2000 crisis worries increase, stressing the food supply chain to the breaking point from which it may never recover."*[6]

Hyatt says that "there are many 'executive orders' already on the books that will allow our president to nationalize all food reserves immediately. *Then you will not be able to buy food reserves. That will be called the crime of 'hoarding!' "*[7] He then goes on to shamelessly pitch his product:

> While some suppliers are taking MONTHS to deliver products to their customers (if they deliver them at all), *the specialized, little known supplier we have found can ship these units RIGHT AWAY.* You can still place an order now and be assured of timely delivery.
>
> But even that won't last forever. Once word gets out that we have a food supplier who guarantees delivery, our phone lines will be jammed day and night. That's why we are making this urgent information available to you, so you can beat the rush. It's my way of thanking you for supporting my efforts to inform people about the coming problems.

But once our phone lines are jammed, then you'd better hope you can live off the land. By then, there may *be no other option, unless you have some other highly barterable commodity.* In my experience though, unless people have bothered to store food, they usually won't store anything else!

Other suppliers are presently selling a one-year, four-person food supply for as much as $6,500 plus shipping! (The fact is, I found one company whose one-year program for four is almost $10,000!) Because over 150,000 people have already bought my book, *The Millennium Bug*, our food supplier knew we could have literally thousands of potential customers. This allowed my staff to negotiate the lowest price I have seen to date on such a high quality food supply. You can receive this *one-year, four-person package for only $3,395 plus shipping!* That's hundreds of dollars lower than other comparable packages being sold to families concerned about the Millennium Bug.

Please order today because after January 1, 1999, when public awareness of the Year 2000 crisis will be at an all-time high, the demand for low-priced food storage programs will naturally skyrocket. (That's assuming, of course, that supplies are still available and IF a national emergency has not been declared which effectively keeps anyone from preparing.) *Please act now to protect your family while supplies are still available!*

A Final Thought on Food Storage

Even if there are just two of you or you feel that the Millennium Bug will never be more than a brownout and last only a few weeks or so, *I urge you to purchase the full one-year, four-person package.* You MUST have enough food to allow you to rebuild your life and help those who have been unable to prepare. You don't want to turn friends and neighbors into adversaries by turning them away in their hour of need. And you also MUST know how to use any surplus food supplies for barter. Because the IRS has virtually declared war on barter organizations in the last decade, very few people have any idea about how to even start bartering. Most of us have lost the barter skills we had as children when we bartered for gum and marbles! But when your resources are at a minimum and your needs for life-sustaining medicines or other items are at a premium, *you must know how to barter!* Because of that I have secured several hundred copies of Phil Hunter's excellent manual *Bartering Secrets*. It sells for *$49* plus shipping and handling. And, I have arranged for anyone purchasing the one-year, four-person package to receive this manual *for free*. Supplies of this manual are limited, so <u>order now</u> to be sure you get your copy. It will take approximately nine to ten weeks to receive delivery of your food, but we'll ship the manual right away so you can start honing up on your bartering skills, right now! Whatever food you buy, wherever you get it, please do something right away!

If you are convinced that you need only a one-year, one-person food supply (this would also work as a two person/six month supply), our food supplier has developed a high-variety low-moisture food package as well. This will need to be supplemented with what you are buying locally. This package, which provides 1,200 calories and 36 grams of protein per day, is available for only $895 plus shipping. (Remember: you must supplement this with other local purchases!) Order one or. . . .[8]

Don McAlvany

Michael Hyatt is not alone in selling fear. Don McAlvany suggests the possibility "that a power-hungry Clinton administration could use the [Y2K] crisis to try to usurp a tremendous amount of financial and political power, much as Franklin Roosevelt did in 1933 in the midst of the Great Depression."[9] Says McAlvany, "Clinton/Gore and their Establishment comrades may be intentionally setting the stage for a panic and the declaration of a state of national emergency and martial law sometime in 1999."[10] McAlvany goes on to speculate:

> Is it possible that they will use this "emergency" to further their agenda, to attack and silence the right wing as they did after the Oklahoma City bombing, push gun control, and other people-control measures that would never get through Congress or be accepted by the people in normal times? Could it be that they have no intention for national elections to be held in 2000 because Bill, Al, and Hillary see themselves as "more permanent-type leaders" for America in the new millennium?[11]

Such fearmongering is vintage McAlvany and comes as no surprise to anyone who has taken even a cursory look at his materials. What is shocking, however, is that he is now being quoted as a credible source on Y2K by mainstream evangelical leaders such as Dr. Kennedy.[12]

McAlvany's solution to safeguarding against the "Clintonistas,"[13] as he calls the Clinton administration, the "Y2K crisis," and the potential "collapse [of] our international economy"[14] involves storing up silver and gold.[15] In virtually every issue of the *McAlvany Intelligence Advisor* newsletter (*MIA*), he disseminates "anti-government propaganda, unsubstantiated rumor, misinformation, and faulty speculation about the NWO [New World Order]."[16]

Chuck Missler

Chuck Missler, who like McAlvany is a master at selling fear, fueled the fear that "we won't have elections in the year 2000" during his appearance on *Focus on the Family*.[17] Said Missler,

> There are people in Washington that have the fear that we won't have elections in the year 2000 because the administration that is presently in power will not overlook the opportunity to exploit this politically. We've talked about Y2K technically, we have talked about the implications broadly, economically, the ones that worry me the most personally are the opportunities for political exploitation. . . . What worries me are the executive orders. The powers that are available to the chief executive of the United States are absolute, they are staggering to read through those. And all that is required to invoke those is a stroke of his pen to declare a national emergency.[18]

Fueling fears of governmental conspiracies is part and parcel of the rhetoric of men like Missler. Richard Abanes notes that Missler's July 1995 *Personal Update* insinuates "that the government blew up the federal building in Oklahoma City."[19] Abanes goes on to document that some of the inaccurate information peddled by Missler can actually be traced to sources such as *Spotlight*—a periodical "produced by the quasi-Nazi Liberty Lobby."[20] *Spotlight* "is widely known as the major source of rabidly anti-Semitic propaganda in America";[21] it is "factually unreliable" and "notorious for racist articles and advertisements."[22] In a 1995 article citing *Spotlight*, Missler "claimed that Presidential Directive #25 (PDD#25) 'states that during times of national emergency, complete command and control of the U.S. military would pass from the President to the UN [United Nations].' "[23]

Abanes, however, demonstrates otherwise:

> [Presidential Decision Directive #25] says nothing about placing U.S. military personnel under "complete command and control" of the UN during a national emergency. In fact, it says the very opposite! PDD#25 deals with *peace-keeping* activities of U.S. forces (no mention is made of a national emergency in America). It also provides for changes to U.S. policy that will bring *more*, not less, stringent criteria for participation in peace-keeping activities. It reads: "The policy directive underscores the fact that the President will never relinquish command of U.S. forces."[24]

Just as Missler's contention that during times of national emergency, control of the U.S. military would pass from the president to the United Nations is inherently flawed, so too is his contention that the powers available to the president are absolute. In response to this latter notion, Senator Robert Bennett pointed out that "it would be very difficult, if not impossible, for the federal government to, by executive order, use the Y2K problem, if it is as bad as some people think it might be, as an excuse for that kind of dominance. I think, frankly, there is no real danger of that."[25]

Many other examples could be cited, but suffice it to say, these sensationalists are notorious for peddling factually flawed information. To add insult to injury, the facts they do get right are frequently misinterpreted. Furthermore, fear-selling tactics are frequently self-serving. As amplified by Richard Abanes in *End-Time Visions*, men such as McAlvany are in the business of selling gold and groceries:

> In nearly every issue of *MIA*, he strongly urges readers to buy gold and silver from International Collectors Associates (ICA)—his gold, silver, and rare coin brokerage

"specializing in precious metals and other conservative investments." Gold and silver, he says, "should be aggressively accumulated up to 35 percent of a total investment portfolio." In one issue he claims that buying precious metals is an "insurance policy against the despotic, socialistic, people controlling New World Order oriented actions."

McAlvany has been ICA's president/owner since 1972. This makes for a lucrative, self-perpetuating cycle that begins with *MIA*: (1) warn readers of the coming New World Order; (2) identify precious metals as the chief, practical hope of survival; (3) sell precious metals to frightened subscribers; (4) use the profits to spread more NWO conspiracy theories and induce more panic; and (5) gain more gold/silver customers.[26]

McAlvany, who also just happens to sell "Self-Sufficiency Food . . . Good as Gold,"[27] recommends that people "should have at least one year's supply of dehydrated or freeze-dried food reserves."[28] After suggesting that a two-year supply would be better, he offers the phone number to his brokerage, ICA.[29] Besides having suggested households store "several hundred (or thousand) pounds of staple grains,"[30] McAlvany further recommends that people move to a "rural setting, a few hundred miles from a large city, that provides a well and the ability to grow food or obtain food from local farmers."[31] He adds, "Alternate heating and energy sources (a wood stove and a backup generator) are vital."[32]

Abanes points out that McAlvany speculated before 1,200 attendees of a 1993 prophecy conference sponsored by Chuck Missler that Bible-believing Christians "may have to go 'underground' in the next two to five years."[33] Y2K simply renews the urgency, said McAlvany: "I have long advocated moving to the country or a small town for many reasons, but the potential upheaval from Y2K problems now makes such a move more important than ever."[34]

The real tragedy is not that men like Hyatt, McAlvany, and Missler are using Y2K as the pretext for selling fear—they've been promoting fear-engendering conspiracy theories for years. Rather, the real tragedy is that their merchandise, messages, and manuscripts are now being promoted by mainstream ministers and ministries.

Chapter 3

Sloppy Journalism

Prior to spending thousands of dollars on Hyatt's food storage plan, buying McAlvany's gold, or investing in Missler's seminars and sermons, I decided to check out their stories and statistics. Sadly, such investigative journalism has become a virtual dinosaur in the Christian community. As a result, sloppy journalism has been allowed to run wild.

Centenarian Kindergartener

A classic case in point is found in *The Millennium Bug*. There, Michael Hyatt points out that one need not wait until the year 2000 to see warning signs of things to come. He reports one of these warning signs as follows: "In Kansas, a 104-year-old woman was given a notice to enter kindergarten."[1] On his videotape series with John Ankerberg, Chuck Missler repeated Hyatt's words verbatim. Said Missler, *"In Kansas, a 104-year-old woman was given a notice to enter kindergarten."*[2]

I was somewhat suspicious of the story because I had originally heard Dr. D. James Kennedy tell a remarkably similar story. In Dr. Kennedy's version, however, the 104-year-old woman was not from *Kansas* but from *Minnesota*.[3] In addition, Kennedy reports that the notice to enroll in kindergarten came *"from the government."*[4]

Sensationalist Grant Jeffrey added his own unique twist to the tale. According to Jeffrey, "A 104-year-old woman recently received a letter from the school board advising her that she must be prepared to start school the following year." Jeffrey, however, claims that the woman is neither from Minnesota nor from Kansas—rather, she is from *Michigan*.[5] In a later version of the story, Jeffrey changed the state from Michigan to Minnesota and added the assertion that the 104-year-old woman received her letter *"from the Minnesota Department of Educational* [sic]."[6]

First, I was struck by the fact that this story is being used as an example of "the world laid low by two lousy digits."[7] In reality, it's a classic case of making a mountain out of a molehill. While there was a centenarian in Minnesota (not Kansas or Michigan) who received a notice from the local Roman Catholic school system (not the government or the Minnesota Department of Education) to enroll in kindergarten in 1993, the letter was not sent out due to a computer glitch but due to a human error.[8] Betty Mullen, the secretary for the St. Stanislaus Kostka Parish in Winona, Minnesota, spotted the error and used her "Y2K compliant pen" to cross out the name of Mary A. Bandar, born June 2, 1888.[9] Despite the fact that Bandar's name was crossed off the list, the enrollment letter was inadvertently sent out by the Roman Catholic school system.[10]

Furthermore, in researching this story I discovered that Hyatt was repeating an erroneous report from a 1997 *Newsweek* article;[11] that Missler copied Hyatt's story;[12] and that a host of others had added embellishments along the way. Sadly, long after I informed Hyatt of his faulty conclusions, he continued to circulate the story complete with the original errors.[13]

Finally, according to Betty Mullen, the parish secretary, not one of the Christian leaders circulating the story concerning the centenarian had bothered to contact her to check out the facts before repeating them.[14]

While a fallacious report concerning a centenarian may not prove to be particularly harmful, one of the other Y2K stories currently circulated by Christian leaders could have devasting consequences for a company. This story, involving the destruction of tons of corned beef, is used by Y2K sensationalists to further bolster the contention of a coming "catastrophe."

Corned Beef Caper

Michael Hyatt assured staff members of Focus on the Family that they did not have to wait until the year 2000 to get a glimpse of what the future holds. Said Hyatt: "There was a story about Marks & Anderson, a firm in Great Britain, whose computers ordered the destruction of tons of corned beef because it had an expiration date into the next century, and the computer thought that it had expired at the beginning of this century."[15] Once again, however, Hyatt and those who are repeating his fallacious story are woefully wrong.

First, the assertion that tons of corned beef were destroyed is patently false. Sue Sadler, who was corporate press officer for Marks & Spencer at the time of the incident in the fall of 1996, explained that "computers had *not* ordered the destruction of tons of corned beef." In fact, no corned beef had been destroyed at all![16] To suggest that the staff of Marks & Spencer were so dense that they believed that their corned beef had been produced over 100 years ago is to impugn their intellectual acumen.

Furthermore, the corned beef in question might better be characterized as "tins" rather than tons.[17] Not only that, but the computer did not "think" the corned beef in question was more than 100 years old in the first place. In truth, it simply did not read the date properly. As a result, the cases of corned beef were entered into the computer manually by "a Y2K compliant person" and shipped out as per usual.[18]

Finally, Hyatt did not even get the name of the company right. As correctly communicated by *Newsweek*, the company name is not Marks & Anderson but Marks & Spencer.[19] Sadly, as before, though Hyatt was apprised of his mistakes he continued to circulate his misleading report.[20]

Criminal Contentions

Yet another example of sloppy journalism is the story now being circulated in Christian circles regarding dozens of criminals who were inadvertently released as a foreshadowing of Y2K. Hyatt claims the prisoners were freed from a state prison in Pennsylvania;[21] Jeffrey claims that the "dozens of criminals" were released as the result of a computer glitch in Canada;[22] and Kennedy suggests that prisoner releases happened in more than one prison.[23]

First, it should be noted that this story, like some of the others, can be traced to the *Newsweek* article titled "The Millennium: The Day the World Shuts Down."[24] The Christian Research Institute contacted the two major authors of the article, as well as two of its contributors, none of whom produced the name of the prison(s) in question.[25] One of the contributors said he thought the prison might be located in Sacramento, California. We contacted the two state prisons in the Sacramento area—Sacramento State and Folsom Prisons. Billy Mayfield (public information officer at Sacramento State Prison) and Michele Taylor (public information officer at Folsom) not only confirmed that prisoners had not been released as a result of the millennium bug, but also communicated that to their knowledge no such documented releases had occurred anywhere.[26] In addition, Taylor pointed out that whatever Y2K problems there might have been at Folsom were already resolved.

Furthermore, even if true, hearsay has virtually reduced the story to the status of an urban legend. When I contacted some of the Christian leaders circulating the story I discovered that they couldn't tell me the names or numbers of the prisoners allegedly released much less the name of the prison(s), where the prison(s) are located, and when the prison releases allegedly occurred.[27]

Finally, to suggest that computers could unilaterally release criminals should stretch one's credulity beyond the breaking point. Incredibly, so many people are swallowing such stories that the President's Council on Year 2000 Conversion has been forced to post the following statement:

RUMOR: Y2K problems in Federal prison facilities will cause cell doors and gates to open, increasing the risk of prison escapes.

FALSE. According to the Federal Bureau of Prisons, cell doors and gates in Federal prison facilities do not have Y2K vulnerabilities. Controls on doors and gates are alway managed by corrections officers, and the doors and gates do not operate on timers. Prison doors and gates are opened through human control when the corrections officer pushes a button. In the event of power failures, the doors and gates default to a closed position.[28]

Such unsubstantiated stories circulated by spiritual leaders inevitably give Christianity a black eye. It's one thing for secular sensationalists to spread unsubstantiated stories through the media, it's quite another for those who claim to represent the One who called himself not only the Way and the Life but *the Truth*. It is becoming all too common for those who take the sacred name of Christ upon their lips to spread stories that have little basis in fact.[29]

The consequences to Christianity might best be communicated by revisiting a report circulated worldwide by the Trinity Broadcasting Network (TBN) that scientists had discovered hell in Siberia.[30] According to the story, scientists drilled a hole nine miles into the earth's crust, shoved a microphone into the hole, and heard the voices of thousands—maybe millions—of tormented souls, screaming in agony.

Paul and Jan Crouch, founders of TBN, claimed their tale was documented by major newspaper accounts as well as a letter from a Scandinavian Christian. The documented newspaper account turned out to be nothing more than a fabrication—a sensational story printed by a charismatic Christian tabloid with no factual basis. And the letter? It turned out to be a hoax concocted by a man named Age Rendalin to demonstrate just how easily Christians can be duped.

When Rendalin first heard on TBN that hell had been discovered in Siberia, he decided to have a little fun at the expense of credulous Christians. He wrote the Crouches to tell them that while at first he laughed at their story, upon returning to Norway, he found the newspapers chock-full of documentation on the "hell hole." Rendalin went on to say that tremendous fear took hold of him, and amid dreams and nightmares of hell, he surrendered his life to Christ. Along with his letter, Rendalin provided the Crouches with his "translation" of an article from a large and reputable Scandinavian newspaper, which provided further details on the discovery.

In the translation, Rendalin provided details that should have stretched even the Crouches' credulity beyond the breaking point. For example, the newspaper article allegedly reported the appearance of "a fountainhead of luminous gas shooting up from the drill site. Out of the midst of the luminous gas, a brilliant being with bat wings appeared with the words, 'I have conquered.' "

When contacted by a Christian radio talk show host who was

more interested in communicating truth than circulating tales, Rendalin said, "None of it is true. I fabricated every word of it." Rendalin went on to say, "Religion is no excuse for being careless with the truth. A simple phone call would have been enough to expose the bogus information I supplied. . . . I must confess I share in full the general public's disgust with these media preachers, who long since tired of preaching the Christian gospel, and in its place substituted a *National Enquirer*-style gospel of cheap sensationalism."

While Rendalin's rebuke might well be dismissed by some as mere rhetoric from a reprobate, it is time for Christians to wake up and take notice. It is indeed tragic that the secular world has had to chide those who claim to be followers of Christ, the very personification of truth. While the Crouches may argue that their fabrications are justified because they have borne fruit, we would do well to recognize that the end does not justify the means. Careful examination of the false facts and false fruit they extol often reveals little more than disease, division, and disillusionment.

Just like the hell-hole story, the Y2K tales regarding the centenarian kindergartener, corned beef caper, and computer release of criminals are now being cited as evidence that Christians are easily led as well as willing to promote virtually anything that furthers their cause. Thus, the fruit more often than not is controversy rather than conversion.

Even a random sampling of secular talk shows in America confirms the fact that millions today write off Christianity as little more than a hoax. Their assumption is that Christians who willingly embrace current Y2K mythology are just as prone to embrace "mythology" that is 2,000 years old.

Chapter 4

Sophistry

As with sloppy journalism, Y2K sophistry has become a virtual art form in Christian circles. Sophistry might best be defined as subtly deceptive reasoning or argumentation.[1] At first blush the argument in question appears to be airtight, but on closer examination its flaws are revealed.* An apt illustration is the sophistry used by Chuck Missler to exaggerate what Michael Hyatt refers to as "Y2K's dirty little secret,"[2] namely, embedded chips.

Embedded Chips

In the video series by Chuck Missler and John Ankerberg titled *Will America Survive the Y2K Crisis?*, Missler presents an elaborate argument designed to demonstrate just how vulnerable embedded chips have made our banking system. Says Missler:

---

*While I am arguing that many Christian leaders are deceiving their listeners with respect to Y2K, it may well be the case that many of these men have been deceived themselves on the issue and are not purposefully leading their followers astray.

Another issue is the day of the week. January 1st of 1900 was a Monday. January 1st of the year 2000 is a Saturday. So computers are going to get confused as to what day of the week it is. And this is nontrivial. Many programs need to know what the day of the week it is for various reasons. I'll give you one example and that's these chips that are inside bank vaults, buried in concrete throughout the United States. There are chips that are used to open a bank vault on a Monday but this would be on a Saturday. When a bank is built, they build the vault, they cement it in, and then build the bank around it, and buried in the vault is the chip designed to open it on a Monday. If that chip is confused, it gives an enormous opportunity for a crook to show up on a Saturday who's figured this out. Now the vendor of the bank door has a warranty, but the fine print says all you have to do is send the vault to the vendor and he'll be glad to fix it for you. Of course, this isn't very practical.[3]

Unless you are aware of the facts, Missler's subtly deceptive reasoning may appear to have real substance. While initially impressed, I decided I'd better check out the substance of his story before pulling my money out of the bank. Thus, I consulted several professionals who make and service bank vaults.[4] At first they laughed at Missler's story, but their amusement turned to amazement when they realized that well-respected Christian leaders are actually circulating this sort of sophistry.

First, if you did not know any better, you would think that Missler is an expert on the design of bank vaults. He not only provides a description of where the chip designed to control the opening and closing of the bank vault is buried but he seems to have read the fine print on the vault door warranty as well. In reality, however, it turns out that Missler is woefully misinformed.

Furthermore, I discovered that the opening and closing of bank vaults is not regulated by embedded chips to begin with. Instead, the doors are mechanically operated using triply redundant hand-wound mechanical timers that are set each evening by bank personnel. As one expert retorted, "If there is a chip buried in the cement, it's because it fell out of someone's pocket."[5]

Finally, even if there were embedded chips buried in cement, the notion that these chips unilaterally open and close bank doors on particular days is unadulterated nonsense. Missler's contention that a bank vault would snap open on Saturday making the bank accessible to a crook "who's figured this out" and inaccessible on Monday to customers who haven't is laughable.

What is not so funny is that credible Christian leaders like Dr. D. James Kennedy are now circulating similar stories. Said Kennedy: "January 1 comes on Saturday in 2000, but in 1900, it was Tuesday, so all of the bank vaults may be open or closed when they should be the other way around."[6] [*Author's note: January 1, 1900, was actually a Monday.*]

English Power Plant

To further frighten the uninformed, Y2K sophists are now communicating that the embedded chip problem is of such gravity that already an entire power plant had to be shut down and subsequently abandoned. Grant Jeffrey told devotees, "Recently, a power plant in England had to be shut down, the result of a single chip failure in one of the generators. But the chip is so inaccessible it cannot be replaced, which means that the entire plant will have to be abandoned."[7] Like the bank vault story, Christian leaders are circulating this rumor with their own unique embellishments. Said Missler:

> In Britain, a major 500-megawatt power plant failed. And when they investigated why it failed, they discovered

that in one of the smokestacks there was a sensor with a chip in it that they never realized had a time/date dependency because of the way it takes sampling and the way it was applied.[8]

In reality, it appears that this story has been fabricated out of whole cloth. In contacting the primary purveyors of the story I was not given any tangible information. Instead, I was told that details and descriptions were available in major British newspapers or on credible Internet sites.[9] I discovered to my amazement that this was simply not the case. In fact, a thorough search through the online archives of both the *London Times* and the *London Telegraph* has not revealed a story such as the one suggested by Jeffrey and Missler. A search through the massive Y2K archives on Peter de Jager's website as well as many other sites has yielded equally negative results.[10]

Furthermore, given Jeffrey's track record for communicating erroneous information with regard to everything from earthquakes[11] to equidistant letter sequencing (ELS),[12] it is amazing that credible Christians quote him as though he were a reliable source.

Finally, plain old common sense should be enough to cause one to question the truth of a story suggesting that an entire power plant would be abandoned because a single chip failed in one of its generators. In spite of the facts, this sort of sophistry continues to circulate in Christian circles.

Not long ago, Missler reported yet another embedded chip story:

The Department of Defense conducted Y2K tests on four silos containing missiles with nuclear weapons. When the computer systems were programmed to the year 2000, two missile silos shut down and two fired off their missiles. Thankfully, it was only a simulated test. The problem is, the experts don't know why two silos shut down and the other two fired.[13]

When Steve Hewitt, editor-in-chief of *Christian Computing* magazine, challenged this story, he was told that in reality there was no such Department of Defense report.[14]

Emergencies

Men like Missler appear to be bent on creating a Y2K panic. They tell a story and then postulate a plethora of preposterous "what if" scenarios. In the case of the Department of Defense, Missler intoned, "It is a known fact that much of the same computer software running many of our American programs has been stolen by the Russians and Chinese. What would happen if we were to solve our Y2K computer problems and they didn't?"[15] Such sophistry is now so rampant that emergencies are cropping up behind virtually every bush.

Michael Hyatt has gone so far as to portray a meltdown of society. According to Hyatt, if this scenario comes to pass, "the public will live in a state of terror. In the words of Roberto Vacca, we will be living in a 'new dark age' and all that that will mean: war, famine, and pestilence."[16] Hyatt believes that "we will end up somewhere between the brownout and blackout scenarios."[17] In the former scenario, "not all federal government agencies will make it. The Internal Revenue Service (IRS) in particular will not come close."[18] In the latter scenario, such emergencies will prevail that "we can expect to see the president invoke the Emergency Powers Act."[19] Said Hyatt:

> I think we will see martial law. In essence, the military will be running things. And the IRS? Kiss it goodbye. Its back will finally be broken—at least for several years to come. . . . Because the military will be in such disarray, we

could be vulnerable to foreign invasion. . . . What concerns me is an invasion from a low-tech country with a huge army. Say, for example, *China*. . . . My guess is that citizens will be forced to band together in small neighborhood militia groups. Unfortunately, many of them will be out-gunned by the "bad guys."[20]

First, Hyatt's sophistry seems self-serving to say the least. The more extreme the emergencies he creates the easier it is to sell his food storage progams. One might recall that before April 1, 1999, Hyatt warned the *Focus on the Family* audience about the potential chaos that could result as New York state and Canada began their fiscal years.[21] After April had come and gone, however, he posted an article on his website that read, "The Canadian government, and the New York State government, began their fiscal year 2000 on April 1, 1999. As I write, no problems have been reported. *And that is exactly what should have been expected* [emphasis added]."[22]

Ironically, Hyatt acknowledges in the same article that "Y2K alarmists have been setting themselves up to look stupid, without any help from Y2K skeptics. Harping about 'trigger dates' is the Y2K alarmists' most effective way of shooting themselves in the foot by setting up false bad [*sic*] expectations."[23]

Furthermore, the emergency scenarios created by Hyatt are so bizarre they should make those who recommend him blush with embarrassment. It is one thing to suggest chaos in Canada, it is quite another to suggest an invasion by China. Not only is such a suggestion arbitrary, it is capricious as well. In reality, there is no warrant for suggesting that our military will be in "disarray."[24]

Finally, I should emphasize that as one exaggerated emergency after another evaporates, the line of demarcation between those who are simply misled and those doing the misleading becomes more evident. Exploiters create new emergencies. The exploited confess their error.*

---

*As noted earlier, Dr. Jerry Falwell initially asserted, "The [Y2K] problem cannot be fixed because we do not have enough programmers." Thus, he advised his followers to begin "stockpiling" immediately. Recently, however, he took his Y2K video series out of circulation and stated, "I do not expect it [Y2K] to be as serious as some are projecting, or as I first feared possible." (Jerry Falwell, as quoted in Steve Hewitt, "Dr. Falwell Updates Y2K Stance," retrieved from *Christian Computing* magazine website 7 July 1999 at www.gospelcom.net/ccmag/y2k/falwell.html.)

Likewise, on May 21, 1999, Dr. James Dobson aired another Y2K broadcast. He stated that while "it looked pretty dark" at the time of his October and January broadcasts, he now had reason for optimism. His guest Ron Blue conceded, "Most of the major systems, like electicity, and probably gas and water, and so forth, and even food distribution, most of those problems are close to being solved, if they are not already solved." As of this writing, however, Focus on the Family continues to sell Michael Hyatt's *The Millennium Bug* as well as previous Y2K broadcasts containing the sophistry and sensationalism of Chuck Missler.

Chapter 5

"Scriptorture"

The Scripture-torturing tactics of Y2K alarmists have become so pervasive that I coined the word *Scriptorture* to describe them. Prophetic Scripture passages from Genesis to Revelation are now being invoked to underscore the seriousness of Y2K as well as the necessity of stockpiling. Gordon McDonald, of Chuck Missler's ministry, Koinonia House, defends the torture of Scripture by saying Jesus and the apostles themselves regularly took the Old Testament out of context. Says McDonald:

> We've been charged with taking the Scripture out of context. You know I might add that Jesus and his disciples appeared to do this fairly regularly. If you look at the times that Scripture was quoted in the New Testament out of the Old Testament and then look back at those passages in the Old Testament you'd be hard pressed under the current definition of "taking something out of context" to not see that almost every time that they used those Scriptures it was taken out of context.[1]*

---

*Peter, for example, in his powerful Pentecost proclamation

Thus, according to McDonald, critics have no business criticizing men like Missler when the Messiah himself takes Scripture out of context.

Prophecies

Dr. D. James Kennedy uses the story of Joseph in Genesis 41 as the precedent for preparing for the possibility of a coming famine by "stockpiling" everything from food to flashlights:[2] "Behold, there come seven years of great plenty throughout all the land of Egypt: And there shall arise after them seven years of famine; and all the plenty shall be forgotten in the land of Egypt; and the famine shall consume the land"[3] (vv. 29–30 KJV). Dr. Kennedy goes on to draw a direct parallel between the past Egyptian shortage and the present Y2K situation. Says Kennedy: "You notice that the Egyptians had food to give to the Israelites when they came. You will be hard pressed to witness to people if you are eating and they are not. So I would urge you to do that [begin stockpiling]."[4]

He warns that this stockpiling should take place before "panic begins to set in, as it will sometime before 2000 when the blasé begin to get the word, and there is little stock left."[5] Says Kennedy: "The prudent man would probably want to have water to drink for the next two or three months minimum."[6] He provides

---

quotes prolifically from the Old Testament—referring to the words of both Joel and David. He not only quoted Old Testament passages in context, but the apologetic effect of these Scriptures was so powerful that 3,000 people were transformed. Had Peter not quoted Scripture in context his message would have lacked any epistemological warrant in the minds of his hearers. This same principle applies to the way Christ and the other apostles quoted Old Testament passages both accurately and in context.

a compendium of Scripture passages by quoting conspiracy theorist Don McAlvany:

> God has frequently given warning to people concerning tragic events that were about to befall them.
>
> - The first one we just looked at was the tremendous famine that came upon the whole world and how God, for his own purposes, not only brought this about, but also sent Joseph to interpret the dream to save many people.
> - Before that there was the flood. For 120 years while the Ark was abuilding [*sic*], Noah was preaching, but alas, few people would listen to him and so it was only his family who ultimately were saved. And the Flood came, and the laughter stopped and turned to terror, panic and horror, and all the others died.
> - God gave a warning to Lot through an angel of the coming destruction of Sodom and Gomorrah, and he and his family heeded it and were saved.
> - God gave a warning also to the northern kingdom of Israel—a warning that the Assyrians were going to attack and they needed to repent. But they ignored the warning and the Assyrians came down like the wolf on the flock and carried them away. How long did it take to get back? Was it an inconvenience? It took 2,600 years to get back.
> - God warned His people through Jeremiah that the Babylonians were coming, and they, too, failed to repent! And so 150 years or so later the Babylonians came down and carried them off to Babylon and they wept by the rivers of Babylon.
> - God warned the Israelites when they were in Egypt centuries after Joseph that the "angel of death" was

going to come down and pass through the streets and look at the people in the houses. They heeded that warning and Passover was born and the people were saved.

• Jesus warned His people also in the New Testament that disaster was coming. He says in Luke 19: "The days will come upon you when your enemies will build an embarkment [*sic*] against you and encircle you and hem you in on every side. They will dash you to the ground, you and the children within your walls. They will not leave one stone on another, because you did not recognize the time of God's coming to you" (vv. 43–44).[7]

Kennedy adds emphasis to such warnings by quoting Proverbs 22:3: *"A prudent man sees danger and takes refuge, but the simple keep going and suffer for it."*[8]

Proverbial Warnings

Of all the Scriptures used to lend credence to the doom and gloom scenarios of Y2K alarmists, Proverbs 22:3 is the hands-down favorite. Preachers from Falwell to Farrar see a direct correlation between the millennium bug and Solomon's proverbial warnings. Grant Jeffrey provides a classic case in point. Says Jeffrey:

The book of Proverbs provides a fundamental spiritual principle that we should all take to heart: "A prudent man foreseeth the evil, and hideth himself; but the simple pass on, and are punished (Proverbs 27:12 KJV)." This compelling advice applies to this [Y2K] situation, as well as to all other dangers. The Lord considered this proverb so important that it is repeated again in Proverbs 22:3.[9]

Proverbs, in concert with other Scripture passages, are cited to make essentially the same point. If we heed the warning of God's prophets we may be spared, if we do not we may well suffer severe consequences. Tragically, such Scriptures are being tortured to fit preconceived notions regarding Y2K. Thus, it would behoove us to heed the words of King Solomon in Proverbs 18:17: "The first one to plead his cause seems right, Until his neighbor comes and examines him" (NKJV).

Pretexts

The oft-cited maxim "A text out of context is a pretext" fits the scenarios painted by Y2K alarmists like a glove. The irony of using passages from Proverbs 22 and 27 as a pretext for urging Christians to begin "stockpiling" immediately is that they simply do not fit. Rather, they merely reinforce preconceptions regarding the millennium bug. Instead of fixating on imprudent applications of Proverbs 22 and 27, one wonders whether it might not be more appropriate to heed the warning of Solomon in Proverbs 28:1: "The wicked man flees though no one pursues, but the righteous are as bold as a lion."

First, I should point out that these tortured passages, and others like them, apply only if the dire assessments of Christian leaders with respect to the millennium bug are correct. However, as previously noted, they are fatally flawed. (For further analysis of the true state of Y2K readiness, see chapter 7.) Joseph's prophecy regarding the coming famine; Noah's prediction of a coming flood; the angel's warning of the flaming destruction of Sodom and Gomorrah; Ezekiel's oracles on the judgment of Israel; Jeremiah's pronouncements of judgment against Judah; Moses' warning concerning the "angel of death"; and Jesus' prediction regarding the destruction of Jerusalem, were clearly divine in origin. In sharp contrast, the prophetic pronouncements of Y2K alarmists are clearly human in origin. While Scripture confidently endorses prophets like Noah and Moses it clearly exposes pretenders like North and McAlvany.

Instead of listening to millennial mythology, we would do well to heed the message of Jeremiah: "I did not send these prophets, yet they have run with their message; I did not speak to them, yet they have prophesied" (23:21). Jeremiah was clearly commissioned by God to correctly warn Judah about impending disaster. In sharp contrast, sensationalists like Jeffrey are incorrectly warning people about impending doom on the basis of sloppy journalism, sophistry, and Scriptorture.

Furthermore, the Scriptorturing of passages like Proverbs 27:12 is extremely divisive. The implications of Y2K alarmists are unmistakable. Those who invest their savings on Hyatt's food storage plan, McAlvany's gold, or a never-ending barrage of Y2K seminars are dubbed prudent. Those who do not are demeaned as imprudent simpletons or fools. As mentioned earlier, I have personally experienced the stinging rebuke of Christians who have charged me with "breeding complacency" within the body of Christ. Some go so far as to suggest that not heeding the warnings of God's "prophets" is tantamount to playing Russian roulette with the lives of my wife and eight children.

It is instructive to note that unlike prophecy pundits such as Jeffrey, biblical prophets like Jeremiah did not have to skew Scripture or statistics to make their predictions. *The Millennium Meltdown* provides a classic case in point. Jeffrey uses Y2K as a pretext to regurgitate end-time conspiracy theories currently popular in Christian circles:

> Despite years of warnings and ample time to avert the crisis, the lights will go out in many cities around the world. Many government agencies and businesses will be temporarily crippled. And the stock market and banking systems—institutions as critical to modern life as the gov-

ernment itself—will suffer challenges not experienced since the Great Depression. . . . Moreover, many scholars of Bible prophecy believe that this crisis may hasten the creation of the coming world government that was prophesied to arise in the last days, according to the ancient prophets of the Bible. The Y2K crisis is unique among all of the disasters that have afflicted humanity through the centuries because it is the first catastrophe in history that will arrive precisely on schedule—on January 1, 2000. This appointment with destiny cannot be postponed or avoided.[10]

Jeffrey makes it abundantly clear that his conspiracy speculations are predicated on his own convoluted view of Bible prophecy. In his words:

I will examine this crisis from the perspective of Bible prophecy because my research suggests that this millennium virus may create an international economic crisis that may motivate the governments of the world to declare a state of global emergency. This would provide an unprecedented opportunity for the global elite to argue for the end of national sovereignty and accelerate the move towards global government—a plan they have been working on for the last six decades—by exploiting the fear the Y2K emergency creates within the general population.[11]

While Jeffrey suggests that governments are exploiting Y2K fears, in reality he is the one doing the exploiting. Incredibly, he has gone so far as to speculate that Y2K may well be the very catalyst that paves the road for global government:

The worldwide Y2K economic crisis caused by the simultaneous failure of millions of computers and hundreds of millions of faulty embedded microchips may be the final crisis that will encourage the nations of the world to surrender. The need to establish global standards of computer communications, a possible worldwide common currency, and a new banking system, may eliminate whatever remaining obstacles stand in the way of the global government the Bible prophesies will rise in the last days.[12]

The question is, how does Jeffrey know that we are in the days leading up to the fulfillment of his end-time scenario in the first place? The answer is, he tortures Scripture to get his own unique reading on the signs of the times. One of those signs is earthquakes. Said Jeffrey, "Since AD 1900, the growth in major earthquakes has been relentless":

> From 1900 to 1949 it averaged three major quakes per decade. From 1949 the increase became awesome with 9 killer quakes in the 1950s; 13 in the 60s; 56 in the 1970s and an amazing 74 major quakes in the 1980s. Finally, in the 1990s, as [*sic*] the present rate, we will experience 125 major killer quakes in this decade."[13]

Predictably, Jeffrey not only misreads the signs of the times, he misinterprets Scripture. As documented in a well-researched article in the *Christian Research Journal*, a consensus of global and regional earthquake data as well as a careful reading of Scripture presents a radically different picture. The *Journal* article titled "Are Earthquakes Signs of the End Times?"[14] documents that no obvious trend indicates an abnormal increase in the frequency of large earthquakes during the last half of this century. In fact, graphical plots of global earthquake frequency demonstrate an overall *decrease*.

Not only that, but the Bible does *not* predict a dramatic increase of earthquakes prior to the return of Christ. Christ, in fact, warns against being deceived by false christs and false alarms concerning such things as earthquakes. As the *Journal* article ably demonstrates, the primary point of Christ's birth pain metaphor "was not that pain would increase in intensity but that the joy of the new birth (i.e., salvation and restoration) would follow the present period of suffering":[15]

> The apostle Paul used the birth image in a similar way in Romans 8: 18–25. The present creation—for which salvation has been achieved but not consummated—"waits eagerly for the revealing" of the children of God (v. 19). This period of waiting is metaphorically described as groaning and suffering "the pains of child-birth (*sunodino*)" (v. 22). The point is not that creation's pain is growing worse but that the pain itself (the enduring effects of humanity's fall) provokes eager longing for the new birth (the consummation of salvation).
>
> Paul used the birth image elsewhere to illustrate the abruptness of the arrival of the Day of the Lord. It will be unexpected 'like a thief in the night' and 'like labor pains' on a pregnant woman (1 Thess. 5: 2–3). Paul's two images are reminiscent of the Olivet Discourse (Matt. 24:8, 43–44). Obviously, Paul was not saying here that we can predict our Lord's appearance by noting precursor birth pains.[16]

Ironically, if Jeffrey's biblical interpretations were correct, seismological data demonstrating conclusively that earthquakes are not increasing would be a confirmation that Christ's return is far off rather than near.

Finally, while Christians are busy worrying about *failing* computers, we might better be concerned about *functioning* computers. Christian leaders who clamor about a coming judgment ought to wake up to the fact that our culture is already in the throes of judgment. The shooting tragedy at Columbine High

School in Colorado is merely the latest in a graphic series of wake-up calls. While we are intoxicated by the prospect of wiring the world for the information age, we are losing our souls. Visual stimuli and information bombardment have become a sick substitute for what Proverbs delineates as wisdom and understanding. As we travel down the information highway, it seems that Christians, in concert with the culture, are picking up a bias against rationality and responsibility.

Ted Koppel, host of ABC's *Nightline*, fears that the information industry is "on the verge of becoming a hallucinogenic barrage of images, whose only grammar is pacing, whose principle theme is energy. We are losing our ability to manage ideas; to contemplate, to think."[17]

Not even Christian leaders seem to be immune. Instead of contemplating and clearly teaching Scripture, some are simply torturing Scripture. Rather than being change agents in the culture, it seems we are contributing to what Carl Bernstein characterizes as an "idiot culture": "For the first time in our history the weird and the stupid and the coarse are becoming our cultural norm, even our cultural ideal."[18] Even a cursory look at the Scriptorture that takes place daily on Christian television and Christian websites sadly illustrates Bernstein's sentiment.

Christianity along with the rest of Western civilization is becoming "a monster of decadence" and we are "slouching, not towards Bethlehem, but towards Gomorrah."[19] Even as I write, a headline in *The Orange County Register* screams out, "Children lured to porn on the Net." The article goes on to detail how "online pornographers have begun luring children with a new 'bait and switch' ploy that links sexually explicit sites to cartoon characters and other Web addresses that appeal to the youngest computer users."[20] Tom Brokaw, anchorman of *NBC Nightly News* said it well: "It is not enough to wire the world if you short-circuit the soul."[21]

Chapter 6

Schisms in the Church

There is no question that Y2K has created a schism in the body of Christ. On the one hand, there are those who believe Y2K has been sensationalized. On the other are those who suggest that not sharing their perspective is tantamount to being just plain dumb or in denial.

The Great Divide

On one side of the great divide are leaders like Christian author John Piper, who believes Y2K has been sensationalized. As Piper puts it, "There is something that smells of hypocrisy in the talk about stockpiling supplies in our homes to 'minister' to others in the coming Y2K crisis":

> First, the greatest need on January 1, 2000, will not be basements stocked with food and water and generators, but hearts stocked with the Word of God. You will be fruitful, you will flourish, you will be life-giving not by seeking the very things the world seeks (Matthew 6:32), but by delighting in the Word of God and meditating on it day and night.

What the world will need and does need from the church is the Word of God that fits us to say, "Who shall separate us from the love of Christ? Shall tribulation, or distress, or persecution, or famine, or nakedness, or peril, or sword? . . . In all these things we are more than conquerors through Him who loved us" (Romans 8:35, 37 NKJV).

The other prophetic word about Y2K is this: Nothing is going to happen on January 1, 2000, nothing, that is as bad as what is already happening to persecuted and starving Christians in Sudan. Or to the staggering number of orphans in Malawi and other AIDS-devastated countries of Africa. Or to survivors in Honduras and Nicaragua. Or to lonely, dying old people in . . . skilled care centers . . . who have outlived their families.

There is something that smells of hypocrisy in the talk about stockpiling supplies in our homes to "minister" to others in the coming Y2K crisis when there are more places to minister this very day that are worse crises than anything that is going to happen a year from now. Y2K will happen to someone every day in 1999—many of them within your reach.

Delight yourself in the Word of God, meditate on it day and night and then take the fruit of your life and go minister to the lost and the hungry and the thirsty that are already so many. Then you won't even notice when Y2K happens.[1]

In sharp distinction to Piper, Dr. D. James Kennedy believes that our basements should be stocked with food and water. In fact, he advises his listeners to start "stockpiling" immediately:

The prudent man probably would want to have water to drink for the next two or three months minimum. . . .

You need to begin to stockpile basic foods. . . . You will need lamps and oil for your lamps, flashlights, and many batteries. . . . You want to be sure you have enough currency, whether in the form of dollars or silver or gold coins, that you will be able to continue on for several months if you don't have availability to what money you have in the bank. . . . The great enemy after denial is procrastination. All of these things are only going to get more expensive between now and 2000. . . . People are beginning to wake-up, dear friends, and that awakening down the line somewhere is going to end up in panic.[2]

As we move inexorably closer to the year 2000, the body of Christ is becoming increasingly divided. Those listening to Christian leaders like Piper are inevitably drawn to the conviction that stockpiling is "hypocritical." Those who heed the warnings of pastors like Dr. D. James Kennedy are convinced that "the great enemy after denial is procrastination" and, thus, are making decisions that may well impact the rest of their lives. As Kennedy himself has put it, "Some people will be wiped out. Some people will get rich. It all depends on whether or not you find out or you say, 'Wha' happened?' "[3]

In fairness, it should be emphasized that Dr. Kennedy holds the majority position. His concerns regarding procrastination and denial are echoed by a veritable army of Christian leaders. Chuck Missler, for one, says he is horrified by what he sees as he scans the Christian landscape. Says Missler: "One of the things we discovered, much to our horror, is that most people that are in denial are pastors and Christians."[4] Scripture is frequently quoted to rebuke those who are not stockpiling for their imprudence and procrastination. Pastors and parishioners alike are feeling the heat. *Religion Today* reports that "one congregation ousted its pastor because he was 'not diehard enough' about pre-

paring for Y2K. Another church nearly went through a split because of disagreement over the issue."⁵

The Coming Economic Earthquake

As Christians become increasingly divided over Y2K, it is
time to take a hard look at the basics. The greatest danger most
Christians face is not the millennium bug but the bad financial
advice that is being circulated by an ever-increasing number of
Christian leaders. Larry Burkett provides a classic case in point.
If everyone followed Burkett's advice to stash a month's worth of
cash, the very "economic disaster" he has predicted would become a self-fulfilling prophecy.

Those heeding Burkett's advice would do well to recognize
that he has a history of making dire financial predictions. The
inside cover of his 1991 book, *The Coming Economic Earthquake*,
reads, "The fact is that America faces its greatest financial crisis
in history during the 1990s." In a 1994 audiotape titled, *Our
Economy in Crisis*, he pushed the envelope even further. Said
Burkett: "I believe unequivocally without any question in my
mind or my heart we are headed *for the largest financial collapse
the world has ever seen* . . . when George Bush got elected that's
like being appointed the Captain of the Titanic."

To his credit, Burkett's 1994 prognostications were not vague
generalities. Instead, he seemed perfectly willing to put his credibility on the line. In his words:

> We are going to have a rapid deflation of our economy,
> I believe, over a period of time, two years probably, three,
> perhaps. Before that we'll start printing money and then
> we'll start printing lots of it and then we're going to have
> hyper-inflation. And I don't mean inflation like we saw
> under Jimmy Carter where the inflation rate got 14 or 15

percent a year. It will be 14 or 15 percent a month, and then 20 and then 25 and then 100 percent, and then two [hundred], then five [hundred], and then 1000 percent a month."[6]

Even more unnerving than Burkett's failed predictions is the fact that calling attention to them or offering a dissenting opinion is tantamount to being branded intolerant. Certified financial planner James Paris experienced this firsthand during an appearance on a *Christian Radio* broadcast. Said Paris:

> Unfortunately, we now live in an age that hinders individuals from making basic judgments about right and wrong. The buzzword of the decade has become *tolerance*. Tolerance, as it is practiced today, means that we no longer have the right to make objective judgments or offer dissenting opinions about anything. This newfound lack of objectivity has transformed our nation into a mentality of "do what you feel is right for you." This kind of thinking has very dangerous spiritual implications. . . . Many Christians are plagued by the notion that they should not make objective judgments about our religious leaders and teachers. I remember learning this firsthand while appearing as a guest on a Christian radio program in Denver several years ago. . . . The show erupted into a flame of controversy when the host asked me my opinion of a new Christian financial book that was predicting a complete collapse of the U.S. economy. This book's author, a prominent Christian personality and radio host, has for years been making similar predictions of economic gloom and doom, to no avail.
>
> Among his unorthodox advice, the author suggested that individuals protect themselves from the imminent collapse by withdrawing all of their money from retire-

ment accounts (IRA's, 401k's, 403b's, etc.) to pay off their debts. He suggested this despite the fact that such an action would cause most people to lose between 40 to 50 percent of the money in their accounts to taxes and penalties. Since I was asked, I offered my opinion. I said I disagreed with the sum and substance of the book. I especially disagreed with the part about liquidating retirement accounts. For the remainder of the show I was verbally attacked with the most stinging and acrimonious words you can imagine. I can still remember many of these comments to this day. One caller said, "Who are you to tear down another Christian?" Another exclaimed: "Who are you to judge? The Bible tells us not to judge; what right do you have to say that you are better than anyone else?" One of the strangest comments was: "How can you disagree with this book? You don't know the man's heart, only God does." What I was being told was that I had no right to disagree with this man's prediction of an economic collapse or his wild and dangerous financial advice either. Mind you, this was not a biblical debate, it was economics—plain and simple. Certainly I had the right to offer my opinion respectfully, didn't I?[7]

The answer, of course, is yes. Paris not only has the right to offer his opinion, he has the responsibility to do so. Nobody's teachings are above sound judgment—especially influential leaders. Biblically, authority and accountability go hand in hand (e.g., Luke 12:48). The greater the responsibility one holds, the greater the accountability one has before God and His people.

In the Old Testament, the Israelites were instructed to practice good judgment through inquiring, probing, and thoroughly investigating a teaching or practice (Deuteronomy 13). In the New Testament, the apostle Paul commands the Thessalonians to test all things (1 Thessalonians 5:21–22) and commends the Bereans for testing his teachings in light of Scripture (Acts 17:11). Instead of rebuking them he lauds their character as noble. While the Lord himself cautioned followers not to judge self-righteously (Matthew 7:1–5), He also counseled them to judge rightly (John 7:24).

Christians are frequently uncomfortable with such judgments. They assume that since they are often painful they are also destructive. However, as apologists Bob and Gretchen Passantino explain:

> The "pain" of biblically conducted confrontation produces individual growth (1 Timothy 4:16), encourages others to Christian maturity (1 Timothy 5:19–20), promotes church strength (Ephesians 4:15), and preserves the church's reputation in the world (1 Peter 2:12).[8]

When Christian leaders make public prognostications such as those made by Larry Burkett in *The Coming Economic Earthquake*, it is not only acceptable but necessary to check them out. While Burkett's predictions regarding the economic earthquake of the 1990s have already proven false, Christians who made life decisions based on them are today bearing the consequences. As with his past predictions, Burkett's prognostications regarding Y2K will likely once again be proven false for one simple reason— he does not have his facts straight![9] If indeed his forecast of "economic disaster" is fulfilled, it will not be due to Y2K computer glitches but due to Christian gullibility.

Regardless of what the future holds, however, prudence dictates that we prepare for Y2K as we would for any natural disaster. For example, if one lives in California it would be wise to ascribe to "earthquake preparedness." Interestingly enough, the guidelines the American Red Cross prescribes for earthquake preparedness closely mirror those it prescribes for Y2K.[10]

Sharpening our discernment skills will go a long way toward bridging the emerging schism in the body of Christ. Rather than dividing over fiction, fantasies, and frauds, we will unite on the basis of truth. Not only will discernment serve to inoculate us against flawed financial advice, but it will also protect us against the falsehoods that so permeate Christian thinking. Bob Passantino is particularly concerned about what he calls false appeals to authority. As he puts it:

> We place too much faith in experts. . . . We seem to think that truth gets truer if someone important says it, even if that important person has no knowledge about a particular field of study. Two plus two equals four, no matter whether a mathematician, a zoologist, or a child says it. Conversely, the popular proposition, "People can achieve anything they believe" isn't true whether Shirley MacLaine, Ronald Reagan, or Mother Teresa says it.[11]

Faulty conclusions are also frequently derived from flawed data. Burkett's speculations regarding embedded chips are based on the assumption that "there are probably, in America, an estimated 300 to 350 million of these embedded chips."[12] Missler arrives at his conclusions on the wildly divergent view that there are "50 billion of them in our society."[13] One thing should be obvious, both of them cannot be correct!

It is also instructive to note that people seem to have an odd predilection to viewing reality as they would like to see it rather than as it really is. For example, Burkett sees the possibility of a world without the IRS. Says Burkett: "The IRS as we know it won't exist probably after the year 2000. Lie as they might, they're not going to be compliant."[14] Kennedy expresses a remarkably similar sentiment. As he puts it, "The IRS just completed spending over $4 billion on about a nine- or ten-year overhaul of their computer system and they say it was a total failure.

They have to start all over again. There is no way they are going to be finished in time. The experts say, 'Bye-bye IRS.' "[15]

While the sentiments of these Christian leaders may be popular, they are clearly based on wishful thinking. Far from being the authoritative judgment of "experts," such thinking flies in the face of common sense. In any case, we won't have to wait long to see just how wildly speculative these predictions really are.

In the same vein, Gary North's speculations also have less to do with reality than with how he would like reality to be. As a Calvinistic Reconstructionist, he sees Y2K as an ideal validation for a worldview in which society collapses and Christians emerge victorious out of the smoldering embers.

Dispensationalist Dave Hunt, on the other hand, holds to a worldview that requires a radically different conclusion. Instead of the societal chaos predicted by North, Hunt speculates that "world events will be moving us toward the peace, prosperity, pleasure, and self-confident rejection of any thought of God's judgment which the Bible foretells—not toward a computer collapse and chaos. *That being the case, we have a biblical reason for knowing that the incredible Y2K disaster being trumpeted will not occur.*"[16] In Hunt's view, *only* the rapture can account for worldwide chaos:

> Logically, it is the Rapture itself which alone could produce the worldwide chaos and *terror* necessary to catapult the Antichrist into power. Indeed, *nothing else could*. Even the greatest problems forecast by the most pessimistic prognosticators resulting from Y2K pale into insignificance in contrast to the sudden and *terrifying* disappearance of perhaps 100 million or more from the face of the earth.[17]

Ironically, both North and Hunt are looking at the exact same data yet arrive at vastly different conclusions as a direct result of their eschatological presuppositions. North draws wrong conclusions from wrong evidence, while Hunt arrives at the right conclusion but on the basis of wrong thinking. In reality, Scripture gives us nary a clue as to whether Y2K will or will not happen.

Finally, let me point out that undue pessimism is exacerbating the emerging schism in the church. In his sermon titled "Y2K AND YOU," Kennedy expressed concern that despite the enormity of the Y2K crisis, the typical American remains cavalier. He used his wife as a prime example. When he explained Y2K to her, Kennedy recalls that she responded, "Well, Bill Gates will fix it." Kennedy had to warn her that even Bill Gates admitted, "I can't fix it. It's bigger than I am."[18]

In truth, Gates said nothing of the sort. Long before Kennedy ran his sermon series, Gates wrote an essay on Y2K in which he said, "If everyone pays attention to the right things and does a good job, the New Year celebration will be about what didn't happen. We'll be celebrating the fact that our computers just kept on running."[19] Gates has also communicated that "he expects minimal Y2K problems in the United States." Said Gates: "By and large, the U.S. fixes are in place."[20] Gates has also relegated Y2K to a "minor inconvenience," and said, "It won't be as catastrophic as some people suggest."[21] In fact, Gates says that technology companies are enjoying "a little bit of a windfall" as a result of Y2K.[22] One thing is certain, the actual sentiments communicated by Gates are far different from those attributed to him by Kennedy.[23]

The Silver Bullet

Like Dr. Kennedy, Dr. Jerry Falwell uses his wife as a prime example of how people fall prey to the myth of the silver bullet. According to Falwell, the *number one myth* regarding Y2K is that "someone will come up with a silver bullet at the last moment and solve the whole thing."[24] In reality, there is no warrant for Falwell's undue pessimism. "Silver bullets" are constantly being developed. Back in 1998, Steve Hewitt, editor-in-chief of *Christian Computing* magazine, was providing the body of Christ with details and documentation in this regard:

> Solutions are constantly being developed that cause old projections to be inaccurate. During the month of July, Citibank, NationsBank and others began using a new program from Data Integrity. According to Bob Osmond, a consultant making Year 2000 fixes for Citibank, this latest program has allowed them to fix in one day a system with over 100,000 lines of code. Before this latest fix, it would have taken them 30 days using other tools. More programs and solutions continue to reach the market each week.[25]

In addition to such silver bullets, Bill Gates points out that a host of Y2K problems have been resolved as a direct result of corporations spending billions of dollars to upgrade their computer systems.[26] This will inevitably result in enhanced communications capability and increased productivity. Thus, many top economists see Y2K as an *economic boon* as opposed to an *economic boondoggle*:

> In a survey of 33 top economists done by the Philadelphia Federal Reserve, they concluded that Y2K would not have any negative effects on society. Twenty-nine of them actually stated that Y2K might have positive effects on productivity and our economy because so many businesses have upgraded their computer systems to newer, faster systems. As well, because of the amount of backup contingency plans that have been adopted by so much of our business and government agencies, it is believed that we will see less disruptions of services than we would in times of "business as usual."[27]

Chapter 7

Seven Frequently Asked Y2K Questions

Some of the most frequently asked questions on the *Bible Answer Man* broadcast deal with what could best be described as millennial madness. The changeover in the calendar to the "big number with all the zeros" is spawning a multitude of millennial myths. It is not surprising that these myths have produced a virtual Y2K rumor mill. Rumors are now so pervasive that the President's Council on Year 2000 Conversion has had to issue a rumor alert on their website. The report addresses gossip ranging from failing elevators to malfunctioning pacemakers.[1] Mythology regarding medical devices, telecommunications, and food distribution is particularly prevalent. Thankfully, these rumors have been ably addressed.

First, according to the U.S. Food and Drug Administration (FDA), people can rest assured that "the vast majority of medical devices will function without any potential health or operational problem after December 31, 1999."[2]

Furthermore, according to the Federal Communications Commission (FCC), "Telephone call processing in the U.S. is expected to continue without major disruption from Year 2000-related problems." This report is based on six months of testing by the Telco Year 2000 Forum, "a consortium of the nation's largest local telephone companies, including Ameritech, Bell Atlantic, BellSouth, Cincinnati Bell, GTE, SBC Communications, and US West."[3]

Finally, Y2K czar John Koskinen has made it abundantly clear that "government agencies and trade organizations representing each part of the food supply system have been working aggressively and successfully to address the Y2K problem . . . thereby ensuring the normal production, processing, distribution, and sales of food."[4]

In the following pages I will tackle a number of other frequently asked questions spawned by Y2K mythology, including questions concerning electrical power, banking/finance, and transportation/air travel. We begin with perhaps the most common question of all—namely what is the millennium bug?

(1) Define Y2K or what is popularly referred to as the millennium bug.

Simply stated, Y2K stands for "Year 2000." The Y2K problem can be traced back to a programming tradition in which two rather than four digits were used to represent a given year. 1950, for example, was electronically stored as 50. Dr. D. James Kennedy explains:

> Nobody, it seems, in all of Nerd-dom thought about what would happen in the year 2000. That's not completely fair or accurate. Some did, but they believed that these computer programs they were writing 40 years ago would long have been retired and updated. But many of them are still in use. Thousands of them are going. Billions of them are still going. So now the question is: What does the computer do when "99" meaning to the computer 1999, turns into "00"? The computer will read that as 1900.[5]

Bill Gates is far more charitable in his assessment of what Dr. Kennedy jokingly refers to as "Nerd-dom." As Gates explains, "The two-digit date is a convenience that consumers like. When you go to the doctor's office and fill in your birth date on a form, you instinctively write a two-digit date. It's not surprising that programmers write applications that work the same way we think. This is why even some software written in the late 1990s has the year 2000 problem, although few mainstream PC products do." Furthermore, as explained by Gates:

> The Year 2000 problem is caused by the use in software of two-digit dates, such as "01," to stand for years. When we go from 1999 to 2000, two-digit dates become ambiguous. If you retire in 2001 and the computer interprets "01" as 1901, it could decide that you retired before you were hired and so your pension is zero. . . . It's still unclear how much pain there will be, but companies all over the world are working hard to prevent it. Assisted by computer vendors and consultants, companies are trying to minimize the two-digit problem before 2000 arrives. Mainframes are the most severely affected, in part because two-digit usage was common in older systems where memory was limited due to high costs. . . . Businesses should recheck their existing custom software and ensure that they use four-digit dates in all custom applications in the future. . . . If everyone pays attention to the right things and does a good job, the New Year celebration will be about what didn't happen. We'll be celebrating the fact that our computers just kept on running.[6]

(2) Is Y2K a problem that is spread over time *or is it more correctly a problem focused on a* specific point in time—*namely January 1, 2000?*

In point of fact, Y2K is a problem that is spread over time. We will not have to wait until January 1 to measure the impact of

Y2K. The problems associated with credit card expiration dates, for example, have been largely solved. Other problems have already been dealt with as well. April 1, 1999, was considered to be mission critical in that this was the date on which a number of states began their 2000 fiscal year. Likewise, July 1, 1999, was considered to be crucial in that many corporations and government agencies began fiscal 2000.

As previously noted, in the April 1999 *Tabletalk*—the magazine of R. C. Sproul's Ligonier Ministries—there is a story in which such dates as April, July, August, and September of 1999 are considered crucial. In April, according to the article, several states enter their fiscal year. In spite of the promises, the computers simply lock up. In July, more states experience breakdowns in police, administration, record keeping, welfare, and so forth as the result of computer shutdowns. In August, the global positioning system fails and the government declares martial law. September brings even more severe consequences as computers cannot deal with "9/9/99." In the end, civilization as we know it today, ceases to exist as a result of Y2K.[7]

Because Y2K is a spread-over-time problem, we can already see whether predictions of disaster are coming to pass or have been largely overblown. As of this writing, April 1 has come and gone without the severe consequences predicted. Likewise, July and August have passed without the apocalypse predicted. It is significant to note that the Gartner Group, a highly reputable information technology research and consulting firm, estimates that "only 10 percent of Y2K failures will occur within two weeks of 01/01/2000."[8]

(3) What is the likelihood that power outages will occur as a result of Y2K?

According to Jerry Falwell, "The national power grid, the most important system that controls all of the little and the big computers, the PCs and the mainframes—everything is inter-connected—could go down. And if it goes down because of programming errors throughout the system, some believe that a ten-year depression would be a mild result."[9]

However, as reported by the *Los Angeles Times*, "The chance of widespread power outages in the United States appears slim. The North American Electric Reliability Council, a trade group that coordinates electric utilities across the country, reported that as of the end of March [1999], electric utilities had completed more than 75 percent of their repairs. While there is still the possibility of localized problems, most utilities have taken steps to insure there will be no serious disruptions during the New Year's holidays."[10]

(4) Will it be safe to fly January 1, 2000?

The *Los Angeles Times* reports, "So far, no aircraft manufacturer has found any serious problems related to the year 2000."[11] Boeing, who has been working on the Y2K challenge since the early 1990s, states that "commercial airplanes are minimally affected by the Y2K problem. Following an extensive survey of thousands of airborne systems, only three were found to be date sensitive. *None of them* compromise the safety of flight or operation."[12] Additionally, as the *Los Angeles Times* puts it, "The Federal Aviation Administration has completed repairs on 97 percent of its mission-critical computer systems" and "FAA administrator Jane Garvey has announced her plans to fly coast-to-coast on the roll over to January 1 to demonstrate her confidence in the air traffic control system."[13] Likewise, United Airlines assures travelers that they need not fear flying as a result of Y2K:

> We have taken a very systematic approach to identify and address potential Y2K issues. In excess of 600 employees worldwide have been working on the project along

with external consultants with specialized expertise. Each step has been documented and reviewed by individuals from all levels of the company. We have checked and double-checked our work to make sure nothing has been overlooked. Boeing and Airbus have assured us that our aircraft have no safety of flight issues, and we have been partnering closely with the FAA and others in the industry. Based on the thoroughness of our Y2K project and the assurances we have received from our critical business partners, we are confident we will be ready.[14]

United Airlines' chairman and CEO, Jerry Greenwald, emphasizes,

We will make sure that you experience the start of the new millennium feeling as safe boarding our aircraft as you do every other day of the year. . . . Safety is our number one priority and our driving force, followed by our desire to provide you with the level of service you expect and deserve from us. We will not compromise the trust you have placed in us or the reputation we have worked so hard to earn.[15]

Despite such assurances from the airline industry, Christian leaders seem bent on creating mass hysteria. Christian sensationalist Jack Van Impe warns his constituency "not to fly after December 31, 1999."[16] Dave Hunt reports the reason Van Impe believes it will be dangerous to fly and that Y2K could be the prelude of the final sign before Christ's return is that "we've only had airplanes since the turn of the century and the Bible speaks about Christ coming at a time when men fly like the clouds, Isaiah 60:8. You couldn't have that [300] or 400 years ago, only in our time."[17]

As puzzling as Van Impe's association of Y2K and airplane

failures is Hunt's analysis. Says Hunt: "Isaiah 60:8 [KJV] asks, 'Who are these that fly as a cloud, and as the doves to their windows?' We don't know who they are; Isaiah doesn't tell us. *They could be angels.* But at least they are *flying*, not grounded by Y2K."

This passage has nothing to do with flying airplanes as indicated by Van Impe or flying angels as suggested by Hunt. As *The Bible Knowledge Commentary,* edited by John Walvoord and Roy Zuck, assumes, Isaiah is using a metaphor to communicate the notion of moving in haste.[18] Van Impe and Hunt are plagued by the same problem: They both violate the literal principle of biblical interpretation, which underscores the fact that we are not to take Scripture in a wooden literal sense but rather in the sense in which it is intended.

(5) How will personal items such as curling irons and clock radios be affected by Y2K?

Y2K fearmongers have suggested that everything from your clock radio to your curling iron may fail with the roll over from 1999 to the year 2000. However, as noted by the *Los Angeles Times*, "Of the tens of thousands of digital consumer products tested by their manufacturers, very few have turned up any problems with the year 2000. Sony, for example, has found only one consumer product sold in America, a camcorder from the late 1980s, that has any problems."[19]

(6) Will ATMs be ready for the new millennium?

Dr. D. James Kennedy is so concerned about access to money that he advises his listeners to begin stockpiling immediately. Says Kennedy: "You want to be sure you have enough currency, whether in the form of dollars or silver or gold coins, that you will be able to continue on for several months if you don't have availability to what money you have in the bank."[20] Federal Reserve

Chairman Alan Greenspan urges people to do precisely the opposite. His concern is "a rash of robberies spawned by people keeping too much cash lying around."[21] Greenspan is, however, hopeful that eventually Americans will "see through any media hype and realize there will be no major breakdowns."[22]

The *Los Angeles Times* reports that "ATM network operators such as the Star System, ATM makers, the Federal Reserve, and the Federal Deposit Insurance Corporation (FDIC) all say there will be no problems with the machines. The FDIC's latest year 2000 review found that 97 percent of banks and savings institutions had satisfactorily prepared."[23]

(7) Will banks be ready for the new millennium?

According to sensationalist Grant Jeffrey, the stock market and the banking systems "will suffer challenges not experienced since the Great Depression."[24] In sharp distinction, Federal Reserve governor Edward Kelley says, "We are confident that the overwhelming majority of banks are carefully and thoroughly preparing themselves and that even if problems arise, they can and will be readily handled, and that the financial system will not seize up or crash."[25]

Ron Blue, who was interviewed on the May 21, 1999, edition of *Focus on the Family* agrees. Said Blue: "For years now the banks have been preparing for the year 2000 and they have all types of contingency plans in place for the only real threat to them, and that would be some type of panic. But they're going to be ready technically and they're going to be ready personally for any problems."[26]

Virtually all banks provide customers with encouraging information about Y2K and their money. Bank of America, typical of the industry, provides helpful infomation in the following question/answer format:

Should I take any action regarding my accounts?

No. It is not necessary to take any special action regarding your bank accounts. Your money is safe and secure. Just keep records as you always have. The safest place for your money is in the bank.

What actions can I take to be ready for the year 2000 date change?

You should:

Stay informed. Keep your bank statements and records of your transactions as you always have. If you bank online, make sure your home computer is ready for the year 2000. Most computer and software manufacturers have extensive websites on their products' readiness. Also, copy all your records to a back-up disk. Avoid scam artists who offer to "hold" your money through the year change. The safest place for your money is in the bank.

What arrangements has Bank of America made to provide alternative ways I can access my money in case a disruption occurs over the January 1, 2000, weekend?

In addition to our nationwide network of ATMs, banking centers will be open on the first business day of the new year, January 3, 2000, and some in-store banking centers will be open January 1 and/or January 2, 2000. You can continue to access your funds by check, check card, credit cards, and online banking.

Will my Bank of America ATM card, check card, and credit card with two-digit expiration dates still work? What if I'm out of town and need to use another bank's ATM machine?

Cards with two-digit expiration dates will continue to work as in the past. We began issuing cards with expiration dates beyond 2000 in 1998.

These cards are being handled in accordance with VISA and MasterCard, or other applicable requirements. However, while merchants and manufacturers are working to make their equipment year 2000-ready, the ability to use Bank of America credit and debit cards will depend on the readiness of the merchants' "point-of-sale" card equipment being used. Although we have taken steps to cause our ATM cards to work correctly in our ATMs, we cannot guarantee other institutions' machines will be year 2000-ready, or that other institutions' cards will work well in our machines if the other institution is not also year 2000-ready.

Will my savings or my investment accounts be affected by the year 2000?

Bank of America understands that maintaining the accuracy and security of customer accounts is a key component of maintaining our customers' confidence. In 1997 and 1998, we focused on the testing and modification of major systems that have customer impact. We intend to maintain the readiness of these systems going forward, so that customer account information will not be affected by the year 2000 date change.

I have a Bank of America mortgage/loan with a maturity date beyond 1999. How do I know that my interest payments have been calculated correctly?

Bank of America began addressing this issue even before 1995 to accommodate 30-year mortgage loans. We have tested and are continuing to test our deposit and loan systems, so that interest calculation and payment processes will remain accurate and reliable now and in the future.

Will there be problems with the direct deposit of my salary, Social Security, or other electronic payments each month?

Bank of America continuously maintains compliance with the standards used for processing Social Security and other types of electronic transactions. We are confident that we will be able to process any electronic transactions we receive, provided that these transactions are sent to us in a format that is in compliance with those standards. If you are concerned about the year 2000 status of the information sent to Bank of America by your employer, the Social Security Administration, or another financial institution, we recommend you contact them directly.

Will I be able to access my safe deposit box?

Yes. Ready access to safe deposit boxes is part of Bank of America's customer service quality commitment, and we will honor this commitment to our customers into the year 2000 and beyond.

What if I still have checks with "19___" printed on them in January 2000?

You will still be able to use any checks with "19___" preprinted on them after 2000. We will ask you to strike through the "19" and write "20" in its place. New check orders are currently being printed without a specific year date, to allow customers to use them now and in the future. As we move closer to the year 2000 date, our check vendors will produce checks that are preprinted with "20___".

Will I still be able to get my balances and activity over the phone?

Bank of America places a high priority on maintaining service quality at our 24-Hour Customer Service Centers, and a high standard of service will be maintained throughout 1999 and beyond. We are working with our service providers, including those that provide telephone communications service to us, to promote year 2000 readiness and avoid service issues.

Will my statements be accurate in the year 2000?

We intend for the turn of the century to be a non-event for our customers. In particular, the updating of account information and preparation of accurate statements should not be affected by the year 2000 date change. We have already implemented and tested the necessary process changes. We also will continuously monitor and maintain the programs that control date-related information on statements.

Bank of America processes our payroll. Will our employees get their money in 2000?

Bank of America attempts to comply with all updates to standards used for payroll and other automated transactions. We will notify our customers of any potential changes and support necessary testing. Our product or application support people will gladly work with your Information Systems staff to address concerns or objectives you may have regarding our relationship.

My company's computers interface with Bank of America. Are any changes required?

Bank of America is making its systems Y2K-ready and will communicate appropriately prior to systems changes being made. If your business interfaces with Bank of America and you have questions, please call your normal contact at the bank.[27]

Epilogue

I began this book by carefully examining the Y2K perspectives of Christian leaders who have contributed immeasurably to the health and growth of the evangelical Christian church.

Although I deeply disagree with their publicly stated perspectives on Y2K, my admiration continues unabated. As this material documents, the views of such Christian leaders as Dr. Kennedy, Dr. Falwell, and Dr. Dobson appear to have been skewed by the sensationalistic statements of Michael Hyatt in *The Millennium Bug* and the fearmongering tactics of conspiracy theorists such as Chuck Missler and Don McAlvany.[1]

As we head for the new millennium, it is my deepest desire that those who have made life decisions based on sloppy journalism, sophistry, and Scriptorture will commit themselves to developing the necessary skills to discern wheat from chaff and heat from light. If we do, the next time we face the selling and subjectivism of Christian sensationalists—as we surely will—Christians will be unified around truth rather than divided by error.

Most of all it is my fervent prayer that in the midst of millennial madness you and I will develop an ever-deepening eternal perspective. First, may our prayer be like that of John Wesley: *"I desire to have both heaven and hell ever in my eye, while I stand on this isthmus of life, between two boundless oceans."* [2]

Furthermore, may the words of John Piper be riveted upon the canvas of our consciousness: *"There are more places to minister this very day that are worse crises than anything that is going to happen a year from now. Y2K will happen to someone every day in 1999—many of them within your reach."* [3] In that great assize, may the Lord say of us, "I was hungry and you gave me something to eat, I was thirsty and you gave me something to drink, I was a stranger and you invited me in, I needed clothes and you clothed me, I was sick and you looked after me, I was in prison and you came to visit me" (Matthew 25:35–36).

Finally, may each one of us internalize the eternal perspective presented by our Master in His majestic Sermon on the Mount (Matthew 6:19–34):

> *"Do not store up for yourselves treasures on earth, where moth and rust destroy, and where thieves break in and steal. But store up for yourselves treasures in heaven, where moth and rust do not destroy, and where thieves do not break in and steal. For where your treasure is, there your heart will be also.*
>
> *"The eye is the lamp of the body. If your eyes are good, your whole body will be full of light. But if your eyes are bad, your whole body will be full of darkness. If then the light within you is darkness, how great is that darkness!*
>
> *"No one can serve two masters. Either he will hate the one and love the other, or he will be devoted to the one and despise the other. You cannot serve both God and Money.*
>
> *"Therefore I tell you, do not worry about your life, what you will eat or drink; or about your body, what you will wear. Is not life more important than food, and the body*

more important than clothes? Look at the birds of the air; they do not sow or reap or store away in barns, and yet your heavenly Father feeds them. Are you not much more valuable than they? Who of you by worrying can add a single hour to his life?

"And why do you worry about clothes? See how the lilies of the field grow. They do not labor or spin. Yet I tell you that not even Solomon in all his splendor was dressed like one of these. If that is how God clothes the grass of the field, which is here today and tomorrow is thrown into the fire, will he not much more clothe you, O you of little faith? So do not worry, saying, 'What shall we eat?' or 'What shall we drink?' or 'What shall we wear?' For the pagans run after all these things, and your heavenly Father knows that you need them. But seek first his kingdom and his righteousness, and all these things will be given to you as well. Therefore do not worry about tomorrow, for tomorrow will worry about itself. Each day has enough trouble of its own."

Appendix

Disaster Supplies Kit

The Federal Emergency Management Agency (FEMA) is convinced that Y2K will cause only minor problems. According to FEMA spokesman Marc Wolfson, "Everything that we know indicates that we're not going to have massive disruptions but we may have some local disruptions."[1] As with any potential problem such as a winter storm or an earthquake, FEMA recommends that all households assemble a disaster kit with enough supplies to last at least three days. Their guidelines for a "Disaster Supplies Kit," prepared jointly with the American Red Cross (ARC), are as follows:

Disasters happen anytime and anywhere. And when disaster strikes, you may not have much time to respond. A highway spill or hazardous material could mean evacuation. A winter storm could confine your family at home. An earthquake, flood, tornado, or any other disaster could cut water, electricity, and telephones—for days.

After a disaster, local officials and relief workers will be on the scene, but they cannot reach everyone immediately. You could get help in hours, or it may take days. Would your family be prepared to cope with the emergency until help arrives?

Your family will cope best by preparing for disaster before it strikes. One way to prepare is by assembling a Disaster Supplies Kit. Once disaster hits, you won't have time to shop or search for supplies. But if you've gathered supplies in advance, your family can endure an evacuation or home confinement.

Prepare Your Kit

- Review the checklist below.
- Gather the supplies that are listed. You may need them if your family is confined at home.
- **Place the supplies you'd most likely need for an evacuation in an easy-to-carry container. These supplies are listed with an asterisk (*).**
- There are six basics you should stock for your home: water, food, first aid supplies, clothing and bedding, tools and emergency supplies, and special items. Keep the items that you would most likely need during an evacuation in an easy-to carry container—suggested items are marked with an asterisk (*).

Possible Containers Include—

- A large, covered trash container
- A camping backpack
- A duffel bag

Water

- Store water in plastic containers such as soft drink bottles. Avoid using containers that will decompose or break, such as milk cartons or glass bottles. A normally active person needs to drink at least two quarts of water each day. Hot environments and intense physical activity can double that amount. Children, nursing mothers, and ill people will need more.

- Store one gallon of water per person per day.
- Keep at least a three-day supply of water per person (two quarts for drinking, two quarts for each person in your household for food preparation/sanitation).*

Food

- Store at least a three-day supply of nonperishable food. Select foods that require no refrigeration, preparation or cooking, and little or no water. If you must heat food, pack a can of sterno. Select food items that are compact and lightweight.

*Include a selection of the following foods in your Disaster Supplies Kit: ready-to-eat canned meats, fruits, and vegetables.

First Aid Kit

Assemble a first aid kit for your home and one for each car. A first aid kit* should include:

- Sterile adhesive bandages in assorted sizes
- Assorted sizes of safety pins
- Cleansing agent/soap
- Latex gloves (2 pairs)
- Sunscreen
- 2-inch sterile gauze pads (4–6)
- 4-inch sterile gauze pads (4–6)
- Triangular bandages (3)
- Non-prescription drugs

- 2-inch sterile roller bandages (3 rolls)
- 3-inch sterile roller bandages (3 rolls)
- Scissors
- Tweezers
- Needle
- Moistened towelettes
- Antiseptic
- Thermometer
- Tongue blades (2)
- Tube of petroleum jelly or other lubricant

Non-Prescription Drugs

- Aspirin or nonaspirin pain reliever
- Anti-diarrhea medication
- Antacid (for stomach upset)
- Syrup of Ipecac (use to induce vomiting if advised by the Poison Control Center)
- Laxative
- Activated charcoal (use if advised by the Poison Control Center)

Tools and Supplies

- Mess kits, or paper cups, plates, and plastic utensils*
- Emergency preparedness manual*
- Battery-operated radio and extra batteries*
- Flashlight and extra batteries*
- Cash or traveler's checks, change*
- Non-electric can opener, utility knife*
- Fire extinguisher: small canister ABC type
- Tube tent
- Pliers

- Tape
- Compass
- Matches in a waterproof container
- Aluminum foil
- Plastic storage containers
- Signal flare
- Paper, pencil
- Needles, thread
- Medicine dropper
- Shut-off wrench, to turn off household gas and water
- Whistle
- Plastic sheeting
- Map of the area (for locating shelters)

Sanitation

- Toilet paper, towelettes*
- Soap, liquid detergent*
- Feminine supplies*
- Personal hygiene items*
- Plastic garbage bags, ties (for personal sanitation uses)
- Plastic bucket with tight lid
- Disinfectant
- Household chlorine bleach

Clothing and Bedding

*Include at least one complete change of clothing and footwear per person.

- Sturdy shoes or work boots*
- Rain gear*
- Blankets or sleeping bags*

- Hat and gloves
- Thermal underwear
- Sunglasses

Special Items

- Remember family members with special requirements, such as infants and elderly or disabled persons.

For Baby*

- Formula
- Diapers
- Bottles
- Powdered milk
- Medications

For Adults*

- Heart and high blood pressure medication
- Insulin
- Prescription drugs
- Denture needs
- Contact lenses and supplies
- Extra eyeglasses

Entertainment

- Games and books

Important Family Documents

Keep these records in a waterproof, portable container:

- Will, insurance policies, contracts, deeds, stocks and bonds

- Passports, Social Security cards, immunization records
- Bank account numbers
- Credit card account numbers and companies
- Inventory of valuable household goods, important telephone numbers
- Family records (birth, marriage, death certificates)

- Store your kit in a convenient place known to all family members.
- Keep a smaller version of the Disaster Supplies Kit in the trunk of your car.
- Keep items in airtight plastic bags. Change your stored water supply every six months so it stays fresh. Replace your stored food every six months. Re-think your kit and family needs at least once a year. Replace batteries, update clothes, etc.
- Ask your physician or pharmacist about storing prescription medications.

General Disaster Preparedness Information

- "Your Family Disaster Plan" (ARC 4466)
- "Your Family Disaster Supplies Kit" (ARC 4463)

General Disaster Preparedness Materials for Children

- "Disaster Preparedness Coloring Book" (ARC 2200, English, or ARC 2200S, Spanish) for children ages 3–10.
- "Adventures of the Disaster Dudes" (ARC 5024) video and Presenter's Guide for use by an adult with children in grades 4–6.

To get copies of American Red Cross Community Disaster Education materials, contact your local Red Cross chapter.[2]

Notes

Before You Begin

1. E-mail on file at Christian Research Institute (CRI), 19 February 1999.
2. E-mail on file at CRI, 22 January 1999.
3. Letter on file at CRI, 21 January 1999 (emphasis in original).
4. Letter on file at CRI, November 1998.
5. Ibid. Later Wall Street tests reconfirmed this conclusion. See Melanie Austria Farmer, "Wall Street up to Y2K task," CNET News.com, 30 April 1999, at www.news.com/News/Item/0,4,035899,00.html?st.ne.87. head.
6. Richard Lacayo, "The End of the World As We Know It?" *Time*, 18 January 1999, 67.
7. Ibid., 68.
8. Ibid., 70.
9. Ibid.
10. Ibid., 64.
11. Ibid., 62.
12. Ibid., 68.
13. Tom Junod, "365 Days to the Apocalypse and We Still Don't Know Where to Hide the Jews . . . and other notes from Pat Robertson's Y2K conference," *Esquire* (January 1999): 96–8.
14. Gordon McDonald of Chuck Missler's ministry, Koinonia House, asserts that critics have been unable to respond to real Y2K events like the

"Peach Bottom, New Jersey," nuclear power plant incident that "shut the whole thing down for seven hours." (Gordon McDonald, "Y2K as a Divisive Agent," Audio Central Y2K update message, 21 June 1999, retrieved from website 20 July 1999 at www.audiocentral.com.y2k/y2kreport/default.html.) McDonald's characterization of this incident, however, provides a case study in sloppy journalism. To begin with, the nuclear power plant in question is in Pennsylvania, not New Jersey. Furthermore, as Peco Energy company spokesman Michael Wood emphasized, " 'It wasn't as if everything in the control room shut down.' The problem affected 'two computer monitors in the midst of hundreds of gauges and other instrumentation. . . . The monitoring system was not safety-related' and 'the control room still uses dials and gauges, plus digital instruments that are not open to Y2K problems' " (Leslie J. Nicholson, "Nuclear-Plant Systems Crashed in Peco Y2K Test," *Philadelphia Inquirer*, 9 March 1999, B01). And finally, according to Nuclear Regulatory Commission public affairs officer Neil Sheehan, "The NRC considered the crash a result of human error, not a Y2K problem." As Sheehan aptly stated, "Even though it was Y2K-testing-related, it wasn't Y2K-related" (Nicholson, "Nuclear-Plant Systems Crashed").

Another example of deceptive data recently brought to my attention involves a story chronicled in the July 1999 issue of Missler's ministry magazine. According to ministry spokesman Gordon McDonald, "In the event it is necessary to take emergency action, it becomes quickly apparent that 'turning off' a nuclear power plant is not a simple operation. Once the fuel rods have been removed from the core, it takes a full five months to cool them down to a temperature in which cooling systems are no longer required. This fundamental fact turns out to have far-reaching influences on the decisions of today. In these five months, the plant is dependent upon off-site electrical power. If that power becomes unavailable, maintaining a stable shutdown mode falls to the reliability of backup generators" (Gordon McDonald, "Y2K Update: Dancing with the Genie," *Personal Update,* July 1999, 14). This story by McDonald is classic sophistry. To begin with, as documented by the Nuclear Regulatory Commission, nuclear reactors can be "turned off" in a matter of seconds. Furthermore, the cooling process is measured in days not months. And finally, nuclear reactors are not only equipped with multiple backup generators that are regularly tested but they are safeguarded through the use of redundancy mechanisms. (See the Frequently Asked Questions—particularly questions five and six—of the

Y2K page on the Nuclear Regulatory Commission website at www.nrc.gov/NRC/Y2K/Y2KFAQ.html.)

15. Abraham Kuyper, as quoted in Charles Colson, *Against the Night: Living in the New Dark Ages* (Ann Arbor, Mich.: Servant Books, 1989), 163.

Chapter 1: Seven Christian Leaders and Their Y2K Perspectives

1. D. James Kennedy, "Y2K AND YOU" (Fort Lauderdale: Coral Ridge Presbyterian Church, 17 January 1999), sermon transcript, 2.
2. Ibid.
3. Ibid., 5–6.
4. Ibid., 6.
5. Ibid., 8. Kennedy also prayed concerning Y2K at the close of this sermon: "Father, may we see this as the greatest opportunity for witness that the church has ever faced" (14).
6. Two-part sermon series aired 17 and 24 January 1999 (entitled "Y2K AND YOU" and "Y2K: WHAT CAN WE DO?", respectively); the third part of the television series aired 31 January 1999, which was a documentary produced by Coral Ridge Ministries, entitled "Y2K: No Turning Back."
7. Kennedy, "Y2K AND YOU," 8.
8. Ibid., 8–9.
9. Ibid., 5.
10. Ibid., 10.
11. Ibid.
12. D. James Kennedy, "Y2K: WHAT CAN WE DO?" (Fort Lauderdale: Coral Ridge Presbyterian Church, 24 January 1999), sermon transcript, 7.
13. Michael S. Hyatt, *The Millennium Bug: How to Survive the Coming Chaos* (Washington, D.C.: Regnery Publishing, 1998), front cover flap.
14. Ibid., back cover.
15. Kennedy, "Y2K: WHAT CAN WE DO?" 5 (emphasis in original).
16. Ibid., 10.
17. Ibid., 11.
18. Ibid., 11–14.
19. Ibid., 1 (emphasis in original).
20. Ibid., 13–14 (emphasis in original).
21. Jerry Falwell delivered this three-part series of sermons at Thomas

Road Baptist Church, Lynchburg, VA, 30 August and 6 September 1998.

22. Jerry Falwell, "Y2K Computer Crisis" (Part I), (Lynchburg, VA: Thomas Road Baptist Church, 30 August 1998), sermon transcript.

23. Falwell, "Y2K Computer Crisis" (Part III), (Lynchburg, VA: Thomas Road Baptist Church, 6 September 1998), sermon transript; cf. Falwell, "Y2K Computer Crisis" (Part I).

24. Falwell, "Y2K Computer Crisis" (Part I).

25. Ibid. (emphasis in original).

26. Falwell, "Y2K Computer Crisis" (Part II), (Lynchburg, VA: Thomas Road Baptist Church, 30 August 1998), sermon transcript.

27. Ibid.

28. Ibid.

29. Ibid.

30. Falwell, "Y2K Computer Crisis" (Part III).

31. Ibid.

32. Falwell, "Y2K Computer Crisis" (Part I); Falwell read verbatim to his congregation this portion of the back cover of Hyatt's book. Cf. Falwell, "Y2K Computer Crisis" (Part II).

33. Hyatt, *The Millennium Bug*, back cover.

34. Falwell, "Y2K Computer Crisis" (Part II).

35. Focus on the Family, "Y2K: Expectations and Preparations (Panel)," 1999, audiotape #CT149/22060 (from the *Focus on the Family* broadcast aired 23 October 1998). Michael Hyatt uses these same terms to describe "Three Scenarios That Could Possibly Result from the Year 2000 Computer Crisis" (Hyatt, *The Millennium Bug*, 159). Hyatt concludes, "I think we will end up somewhere between the Brownout and Blackout scenarios" (180).

36. Focus on the Family aired these radio broadcasts on 21, 22, and 23 October 1998, during which James Dobson hosted a panel discussion on Y2K featuring Michael Hyatt, Shaunti Feldhahn, Chuck Missler, Steve Hewitt, and Ron Blue.

37. Focus on the Family aired this chapel meeting 11 and 12 January 1999. Focus on the Family has since aired another broadcast on Y2K featuring Ron Blue (21 May 1999). During the broadcast, Dr. Dobson conveyed that he has more reason to be optimistic than he was during the October and January broadcasts. Ron Blue also conceded, "Most of the major systems, like electricity, and probably gas, and water, and so forth, and even food distribution, most of those problems are close to being solved, if they are not already solved." Focus on the Family continues to promote

Michael Hyatt's *The Millennium Bug* and offers tapes of their previous Y2K broadcasts.

38. Focus on the Family, "Planning for Y2K (Michael Hyatt)," 1999, audiotape #CT162/22338.

39. Focus on the Family, "Y2K: Expectations and Preparations (Panel)," (portion aired 21 October 1998).

40. Focus on the Family, "Planning for Y2K (Michael Hyatt)."

41. Ibid., (emphasis added).

42. Hyatt, *The Millennium Bug*, 8. Hyatt's actual words before the Focus on the Family staff were: "There was a story about Marks & Anderson, a firm in Great Britain, whose computers ordered the destruction of tons of corned beef because it had an expiration date into the next century, and the computer thought that it had expired at the beginning of this century" (Focus on the Family, "Planning for Y2K [Michael Hyatt]").

43. Focus on the Family, "Planning for Y2K (Michael Hyatt)."

44. Ibid.

45. Ibid.

46. Ibid. In his book, Hyatt warns about "bank runs . . . in which people rush to their banks to withdraw the cash value of their accounts. If enough people do this, the demand will exceed the bank's available cash" (*The Millennium Bug*, 86–7).

47. Focus on the Family, "Planning for Y2K (Michael Hyatt)."

48. Ibid.

49. Ibid.

50. Focus on the Family, "Y2K: Expectations and Preparations (Panel)," (from portion aired 21 October 1998).

51. Ibid., (from portion aired 22 October 1998); cf. website posting on The Ankerberg Theological Research Institute's website at www.ankerberg.com/current%20events.html (as of 23 February 1999).

52. Larry Burkett at "Y2K: Facing the Challenge," the National Religious Broadcasters Convention—1999, 2 February 1999, audiotape transcript.

53. Ibid.

54. Ibid.

55. Chuck Missler at "Y2K: Facing the Challenge," the National Religious Broadcasters Convention—1999, 2 February 1999, audiotape transcript.

56. Ibid.

57. Ibid.

58. Speaker not identified, "Y2K: Facing the Challenge," the National Religious Broadcasters Convention—1999, 2 February 1999, audiotape transcript.

59. Bob Allen at "Y2K: Facing the Challenge," the National Religious Broadcasters Convention—1999, 2 February 1999, audiotape transcript.

60. Ibid.

61. Ibid.

62. Ibid.

63. Steve Farrar, *Spiritual Survival During the Y2K Crisis* (Nashville: Thomas Nelson Publishers, 1999), About the Author.

64. Steve Farrar, "God, Y2K, and You," (San Antonio: Oak Hills Church of Christ, 8 November 1998), audiotape transcript.

65. Ibid.

66. Grant R. Jeffrey, *The Millennium Meltdown: The Year 2000 Computer Crisis* (Toronto: Frontier Research Publications, 1998), 9.

67. Ibid., 10.

68. Ibid., 25.

69. Ibid.

70. Grant R. Jeffrey, *The Millennium Meltdown: The Year 2000 Computer Crisis* (Toronto: Frontier Research Publications, 1999), videotape.

71. Jeffrey, *The Millennium Meltdown* (1998), 25–26.

72. Ibid., 242.

73. R. C. Sproul, "Taking Thought for Tomorrow" (*Tabletalk*, April 1999): 6.

74. Ibid., 7.

75. Ibid.

76. Franklin Sanders, "The Great Collapse" (*Tabletalk,* April 1999): 8–10, 56.

77. Gary North, Institute for Christian Economics (ICE) Newsletter, November 1998, 7.

78. Ibid., 1, 6, 7.

79. See Gary North's website at www.garynorth.com.

Chapter 2: Selling Fear

1. Michael Hyatt has published widely on Y2K, with three books, a large website, and multiple articles. The books include *The Y2K Personal Survival Guide* (Washington, D.C.: Regnery Publishing, 1999); and, co-

authored with George Grant, *Y2K: The Day the World Shut Down* (Dallas: Word Publishing, 1998).

2. Hyatt writes: "Finally, Dr. Gary North, whose Web site literally made this book [*The Millennium Bug*] possible. He collected hundreds, if not thousands, of articles related to the Year 2000 Problem, which made my own research immeasurably easier. If by some miracle the problem is fixed in time and we somehow manage to avoid the meltdown of our society, it will be due in large part to the foresight of this watchman who sounded the trumpet when others were silent and spread the word on the Internet" (*The Millennium Bug*, 274–5). While Hyatt acknowledges his great indebtedness to North, Missler calls North's Y2K views "very extreme" (Chuck Missler and John Ankerberg, *Will America Survive the Y2K Crisis?* [Coeur d'Alene, Idaho: Koinonia House, n.d.], videotape set).

3. Farrar, "God, Y2K, and You." In his own book, Farrar writes that Hyatt's *The Millennium Bug* is "the best one-volume explanation of Y2K that is available" (Farrar, *Spiritual Survival During the Y2K Crisis*, 235).

4. Kennedy, "Y2K: WHAT CAN WE DO?" 7.

5. Michael Hyatt, "A Personal Message About Y2K & Food from Michael Hyatt," retrieved from website 6 May 1999 at http://www.michaelhyatt.com/foodmessage.htm (emphasis is original).

6. Ibid.

7. Ibid.

8. Ibid.

9. Donald S. McAlvany, *The Y2K Tidal Wave* (Toronto: Frontier Research Publications, 1999), 11.

10. Ibid., 234.

11. Ibid., 234–5.

12. Kennedy, "Y2K: WHAT CAN WE DO?" 3, 5.

13. McAlvany refers to the Clinton Administration as the "Clintonistas" (Don McAlvany, "Terminating the U.S. Constitution: The Conference of States," *McAlvany Intelligence Advisor* [April 1995]: 3, 23, 27, as cited in Richard Abanes, *End-Time Visions* [Nashville: Broadman & Holman Publishers, 1998], 145).

14. McAlvany, *The Y2K Tidal Wave*, back cover.

15. Ibid., 245, 247; see also Don McAlvany, "January 1, 2000: Time Is Running Out!" International Collectors Associates' advertisement flier, n.d.; "Life After Y2K," advertisement flier, n.d. Cf. Abanes, 145.

16. Abanes, 143.

17. Focus on the Family, "Y2K: Expectations and Preparations (Panel)," (portion aired 22 October 1998).
18. Ibid.
19. Abanes, 138. See Chuck Missler, "Clear and Present Danger," *Personal Update,* July 1995, 6–9.
20. Ibid.
21. Ibid.
22. Ibid., 139.
23. Ibid., 140. See Chuck Missler, "Constitution A Crime?" *Personal Update*, November 1995, 3.
24. Abanes, 140–1.
25. *Point of View* radio broadcast with Marlin Maddoux, "Y2K and Martial Law," 25 January 1999, audiotape. Senator Bennett's reference to "that kind of dominance" concerned specifically the specter of martial law arising from the federal level. (Senator Bennett, of Utah, is Chairman of the United States Senate Special Committee on the Year 2000 Technology Problem.)
26. Abanes, 145–6.
27. Don McAlvany, "Y2K and Beyond: Don't Get Caught Without Critical Supplies!" advertisement flier, n.d.
28. McAlvany, *The Y2K Tidal Wave*, 247.
29. Ibid., 247–8.
30. Don McAlvany, "Toward a Soviet America: Strangling Americans' Freedom and Constitution," *McAlvany Intelligence Advisor*, August 1995, 28, as quoted in Abanes, 146.
31. McAlvany, *The Y2K Tidal Wave*, 245.
32. Ibid.
33. Abanes, 146.
34. McAlvany, *The Y2K Tidal Wave*, 244.

Chapter 3: Sloppy Journalism

1. Hyatt, *The Millennium Bug*, 9; cf. back cover.
2. Missler and Ankerberg, *Will America Survive the Y2K Crisis?* (Coeur d'Alene, Idaho: Koinonia House, 1998, videotape 1 of 2; emphasis added.) Missler revealed during our phone conversation 23 February 1999 that Hyatt was his source here.
3. Kennedy, "Y2K AND YOU," 5.
4. Ibid.

5. Jeffrey, *The Millennium Meltdown* (1999).

6. "The Millennium Meltdown" on Jeffrey's website at http://www.grantjeffrey.com/article/meltart.htm (retrieved 5 April 1999). Furthermore, Jeffrey makes several other errors in detail. For example, in this ostensibly updated website article, Jeffrey incorrectly reports Mary Bandar's birth date as 1889; and in his video, Jeffrey states that "the school district computer had correctly calculated that from her date of birth she should be starting school in 1900."

7. Hyatt, *The Millennium Bug*, 8. Steven Levy and Katie Hafner, "The Millennium: The Day the World Shuts Down," *Newsweek*, 2 June 1997, 54, at http://newsweek.com/nw-srv/issue/22_97a/printed/us/fty0122.htm.

8. Phone conversations with Betty Mullen, 9 March and 5 April 1999. Cf. "Right year, wrong century: Woman, 104, on kindergarten list," *The LaCrosse Tribune*, 29 March 1993, n.p.

9. Fax confirming Bandar's birth date from Mullen, 14 June 1999.

10. Phone conversations with Mullen, 9 March and 5 April 1999. St. Mary's Elementary School, which is part of the Winona Area Catholic Schools, sent Bandar the invitation. School secretary Kathy Gerth confirms that the letter was inadvertently sent out despite Mullen's efforts to strike Bandar's name off the list. Gerth also confirms that no member of the media has contacted her or the school since the event was first reported in the Winona area media (phone conversation with Gerth 15 June 1999).

11. Levy and Hafner. This article reported: "In Kansas, a 104-year-old woman was given a notice to enter kindergarten."

12. Phone conversation with Missler, 23 February 1999.

13. Phone conversation with Hyatt, 2 March 1999. However, as of 20 April 1999, his website retained erroneous details on this story (Michael Hyatt, "Y2K—Media Briefing—Examples," at www.michaelhyatt.com/briefing/examples.htm). As of 22 July 1999, this misinformation remains at http://www.michaelhyatt.com/survival/xappendixa.htm. (Copy on file.)

14. Phone conversations with Mullen, 5 April and 14 June 1999.

15. Focus on the Family, "Planning for Y2K (Michael Hyatt)." Cf. *The Millennium Bug*, 8.

16. Phone conversation with Sadler, 24 February 1999. At the time of the incident, Sadler was the only press officer commenting on this issue for Marks & Spencer; she is now one of their food press and public relations officers.

17. Per Sadler, the total weight in question amounted to far less than one ton. Chris Burridge, food press officer for Marks & Spencer, also confirmed for CRI that the beef involved was packaged in small tin containers with the total weight being far less than a single ton (phone conversation 19 February 1999).

18. Phone conversation with Sadler, 24 February 1999.

19. See Levy and Hafner.

20. See Michael Hyatt, "Frequently Asked Questions," at www.michaelhyatt.com/faqs/faq1.htm (retrieved 11 June 1999).

21. Michael Hyatt, "Y2K Personal Survival Guide: Appendix A (An Overview of Y2K)," at www.michaelhyatt.com/survival/appendixa.htm (as of 11 June 1999).

22. Jeffrey, *The Millennium Meltdown* (1999). On his website, Jeffrey states, "In one case, a faulty computer program could not correctly calculate the dates for court dates and therefore caused criminals to be inadvertently released (*Toronto Star*, March 30, 1998)" (retrieved 5 April 1999 from www.grantjeffrey.com/article/meltart.htm). I traced Jeffrey's latter reference to the Opinion page of the 30 March 1998 *The Toronto Star*: "In other cases around the world, customers of a financial firm have been billed for 96 years of interest on accounts, criminals skipped after a law enforcement computer refused to file court dates and, in a new version of serving time, one British company is thinking of using prisoners for the drudgery of correcting errant computer code" (Colin Vaughn, "City task force on hunt for computer bug repellant," *The Toronto Star*, 30 March 1998, A15). But the editorial gave no further references.

23. Kennedy, "Y2K AND YOU," 10.

24. Levy and Hafner.

25. E-mails on file from authors in response to CRI's inquiries, 17, 19, 26 February 1999. Phone conversation with one contributing author 17 February 1999. As well, CRI placed multiple voice-mail messages (unreturned) for one writer who left *Newsweek* (e.g., 3 March 1999). These authors also did not confirm other important facts (e.g. 104-year-old woman, corned beef), which were relayed in their article and have been repeated by evangelical leaders such as D. James Kennedy, Jerry Falwell, and Michael Hyatt.

26. Phone conversation with Mayfield, 2 March 1999; phone conversation with Taylor, 6 April 1999.

27. Phone conversation with Hyatt, 2 March 1999; phone conversation with

Missler, 23 February 1999; Jeffrey has not responded to our phone inquiry of 25 March 1999.

28. "Y2K Rumors," President's Council on Year 2000 Conversion website at www.y2k.gov/java/whatsnew1.html.

29. Another irresponsible claim on the cover of Hyatt's *The Millennium Bug* is the following Y2K "warning sign": "An electric utility ran a series of tests on the city power grid to see what would happen on January 1, 2000. The power system simple stopped working" (see also p. 8). In response, a spokesman for Hawaiian Electric (the utility company Hyatt impugns) told CRI that this statement was "absolutely wrong" in that it gave the appearance that customers lost power, which never happened. Furthermore, far from being a foreshadowing of a Y2K catastrophe, this serves as a sterling example of Hawaiian Electric's commitment to Y2K compliancy. Finally, it should be noted that Hawaiian Electric has had to bear the brunt of Hyatt's irresponsibility. (Phone conversation with Fred Kobashikawa, spokesperson for Hawaiian Electric, 19 February 1999.)

30. Discussion adapted from Hank Hanegraaff, "Frauds, Fictions, Fantasies, and Fabrications," *Christian Research Journal* (Winter 1996): 54–5, 35. See *Praise The Lord*, Trinity Broadcasting Network, 18 October 1990.

Chapter 4: Sophistry

1. *Merriam-Webster's Collegiate Dictionary* (Springfield, Mass.: Merriam-Webster, Inc., 1994), 1121.

2. Focus on the Family, "Planning for Y2K (Michael Hyatt)," (portion aired 11 January 1999).

3. Missler and Ankerberg, *Will America Survive the Y2K Crisis?*

4. CRI contacted Mosler Inc. and Diebold, Inc., two of the largest bank vault manufacturers in the U.S. (e.g., Fred Russo, service supervisor for Mosler Inc., Anaheim, CA, 10 May 1999).

5. Phone conversation with Brad Barms, president of Brad Barms Industries, Riverside, CA (12 May 1999). For twenty years, Barms has been installing and repairing bank vaults.

6. Kennedy, "Y2K AND YOU," 10.

7. Jeffrey, *The Millennium Meltdown* (1999).

8. Missler and Ankerberg, *Will America Survive the Y2K Crisis?* As of 23 February 1999, this story was also posted on The Ankerberg Theological

Research Institute's website at www.ankerberg.com/current%20 events.html.

9. Phone conversation with representative from Missler's ministry, Koinonia House, May 1999. Jeffrey has not responded to our phone inquiry of 25 March 1999.

10. See www.year2000.com.

11. Steven A. Austin and Mark L. Strauss, "Are Earthquakes Signs of the End Times? A Geological and Biblical Response to an Urban Legend," *Christian Research Journal*, 21: 4, 32.

12. Hank Hanegraaff, "Magic Apologetics," *Christian Research Journal* (September/October 1997): 54–5.

13. John Ankerberg and Chuck Missler, "What Is 'The Y2K Problem' and How Should Christians Prepare?" The John Ankerberg Show website at www.ankerberg.com/anky2k.htm (retrieved 23 February 1999).

14. E-mail from Steve Hewitt, 28 April 1999.

15. Ankerberg and Missler, "What Is 'The Y2K Problem' and How Should Christians Prepare?"

16. Hyatt, *The Millennium Bug*, 175.

17. Ibid., 180.

18. Ibid., 165.

19. Ibid., 171.

20. Ibid., 172 (emphasis in original).

21. Focus on the Family, "Planning for Y2K (Michael Hyatt)"; cf. Steve Hewitt, "Y2K—The Challenge Ahead, Part 8," *Christian Computing* (April 1999) at www.gospelcom.net/ccmag/articles/covr499.html.

22. E. L. Core, Y2K Editorial: "Don't Chase the Y2K Red Herrings," 13 April 1999 on Michael Hyatt's website at www.michaelhyatt.com/editorials/ herrings.htm. (Thanks to Steve Hewitt for pointing this out, see "Y2K, The Challenge Ahead, Part 9," *Christian Computing* (May 1999) at www.gospelcom.net/ccmag/articles/covr499.html.)

23. Core, Y2K Editorial: "Don't Chase the Y2K Red Herrings."

24. See "Department of Defense ready for Y2K, says Secretary Cohen," Air Force News (AFPN), 22 July 1999, from the U.S. Air Force Year 2000 Homepage at www.af.mil/news/Jul1999/n19990722_991380.html. See also Nancy Weil, "Global Y2K: The great unknown," CNN, 8 June 1999, at cnn.com/TECH/computing/9906/08/overseas.y2k.id. In addition, CRI has obtained information from classified government sources confirming that China has no capability to invade the U.S. and will experience Y2K problems.

Chapter 5: "Scriptorture"

1. Gordon McDonald, "Y2K as a Divisive Agent," Audio Central Y2K update message, 21 June 1999, retrieved from website 20 July 1999 at www.audiocentral.com/y2k/y2kreport/default.html.
2. See Kennedy, "Y2K: WHAT CAN WE DO?" 13. Additionally, an entire ministry has been formed on the basis of the story of Joseph—Joseph Project 2000, founded by Shaunti Feldhahn.
3. Kennedy, "Y2K AND YOU," 1.
4. Kennedy, "Y2K: WHAT CAN WE DO?" 13.
5. Ibid., 12.
6. Ibid., 13.
7. Ibid., 3–4.
8. Ibid., 1 (emphasis in original).
9. Jeffrey, *The Millennium Meltdown* (1998), 25–6.
10. Ibid., 10.
11. Ibid., 25.
12. Ibid., 171.
13. Grant R. Jeffrey, *Prince of Darkness* (Toronto: Frontier Research Publications, 1994), 310–11; as quoted in Austin and Strauss, 32. Austin and Strauss go on to point out that "Jeffrey gives no information on how a copy of this report can be obtained (author, date, report name, and location)," even though Jeffrey repeatedly offers such statistics in his publications (see Jeffrey, *The Signature of God* [Toronto: Frontier Research Publications, 1996], 194, and *Armageddon: Appointment with Destiny,* rev. ed. [Toronto: Frontier Research Publications, 1997], 251–52).
14. Austin and Strauss, 30–9.
15. Ibid., 37.
16. Ibid.
17. From a speech delivered in October 1985 to the International Radio and Television Society, New York City, as quoted in Os Guinness, *Fit Bodies, Fat Minds* (Grand Rapids, Mich.: Baker Books, 1994), 80.
18. Carl Bernstein, "The Idiot Culture," *The New Republic* (8 June 1992): 24–5, as quoted in Guinness, 70.
19. Robert H. Bork, *Slouching Towards Gomorrah* (New York: Regan Books, 1996), front cover flap.
20. Dawn C. Chmielewski, "children Lured to porn on the Net," *The Orange County Register,* 4 July 1999, Front page.
21. Tom Brokaw, anchorman of *NBC Nightly News*, speaking to graduates

at the College of Santa Fe in New Mexico, as quoted in The Associated Press, "Brokaw: Technology Lets People Down," 16 May 1999.

Chapter 6: Schisms in the Church

1. John Piper, "Meditate on the Word of the Lord Day and Night," 3 January 1999, sermon transcript from website at www.soundofgrace.com/piper99/1–3–99.htm.
2. Kennedy, "Y2K: WHAT CAN WE DO?" 13–14 (emphasis in original).
3. Kennedy, "Y2K AND YOU," 8.
4. Missler, "Y2K: Facing the Challenge."
5. "Y2K: How Should We Then Live?" *Religion Today* (18 September 1998), from website at www.religiontoday.com, reporting the thoughts of Jim Jacobson, president of Christian Freedom International; cf. Steve Hewitt, "Editorial," *Christian Computing* magazine (October 1998), on website at http://www.gospelcom.net/ccmag/y2k/edit1098.html.
6. Larry Burkett, "Our Economy in Crisis," 1994, audiotape. Burkett's predictions regarding hyper-inflation in America in the decade of the '90s have already proven false.
7. James L. Paris, *The Christian Financial Crisis* (Daytona Beach, Fla.: Avatar Publishing Group, Inc., 1999), 1–3.
8. Bob and Gretchen Passantino, "Christians Critizing Christians: Can It Be Biblical?" *Christian Research Journal*, Fall 1992, 39.
9. Burkett has a history of communicating facually unreliable information. Sadly, this is the case whether Burkett is talking elections or economics. In his tape, *Our Economy In Crisis*, Burkett says, "Anybody who thinks that this was not a Christian-founded country knows nothing about history. . . . Up until the 20th century you couldn't even run for a national political office without being a professing Christian. Could not run for office, and certainly could not get elected." Nothing could be further from the truth. Indeed, anyone who knows anything about American history *can* name any number of Americans who ran for or were elected to public office without being a professing Christian—including Thomas Jefferson who was clearly a deist. Burkett's facts are equally flawed when it comes to Y2K economics. Consider for example his remarks concerning the IRS: "The good news is the IRS as we know it won't exist probably after the year 2000. *Lie as they might, they're not going to be compliant.*" Anyone who thinks that the IRS will probably not be in existence after the year 2000 will soon discover that they were deluded.

10. Regarding Y2K, the Red Cross has prepared a Y2K checklist, which includes this advice: "Stock disaster supplies to last several days to a week for yourself and those who live with you. This includes having nonperishable foods, stored water, and ample supply of prescription and nonprescription medications that you regularly use." The Red Cross notes that all of its recommendations for Y2K "make good sense, regardless of the potential problem." (From website at www.redcross.org/disaster/safety/Y2K.html.)

11. Bob Passantino, "Fantasies, Legends, and Heroes," 1990, 6, from the Answers in Action website at www.answers.org/Apologetics/Fantasy.html. Booklet available from Answers in Action, P.O. Box 2067, Costa Mesa, Calif., 92628.

12. Burkett, "Y2K: Facing the Challenge."

13. Missler, "Y2K: Facing the Challenge." Grant Jeffrey surmises that "it is probable that approximately twenty billion micro chips exist throughout the world, and we are adding another ten billion each year" (from Jeffrey's website at www.grantjeffrey.com/article/meltart.htm).

14. Burkett, "Y2K: Facing the Challenge."

15. Kennedy, "Y2K AND YOU," 11.

16. Dave Hunt, *Y2K: A Reasoned Response to Mass Hysteria* (Eugene, Ore.: Harvest House Publishers, 1999, 190 (emphasis added).

17. Hunt, 172.

18. Kennedy, "Y2K AND YOU," 8–9.

19. Bill Gates, "Preparing for the Year 2000," 22 April 1998, from his website at www.microsoft.com/BillGates/columns/1998essay/4–22col.htm.

20. Doug Olenick, "Gates Addresses Y2K and the Future," *Computer Retail Week* (7 December 1998), from website at www.crw.com.

21. Reuters, 12 April 1999, at www.garynorth.com/y2k/DetaiL.cfm/4402. The accuracy of this statement by Bill Gates was confirmed 23 July 1999 by Angie Maddox, a Y2K public relations account representative for Waggener & Edstrom, which represents Microsoft.

22. "Gates: Y2K Fears Overdone," CNNfn, 1 February 1999, from website at cnnfn.com/digitaljam/9902/01/davos_gates/.

23. It seems unlikely that Bill Gates actually made the statement Dr. Kennedy attributes to him. In doing primary source research on the views of Bill Gates regarding Y2K, I could not find a single instance in which Gates makes a comment that is even remotely similar in both content and sentiment to the comment Kennedy ascribes to him. I did find a statement by economist Dr. Edward Yardeni in his prepared testimony

before the Senate Banking, Housing and Urban Affairs Committee, 4 November 1998, in which Yardeni states, "The widespread mantra I hear over and over again is 'Bill Gates will fix it.' The official position of Microsoft is that this is a problem that everyone must fix on his own. It is too big and overwhelming for even Microsoft" (from Yardeni's website at www.yardeni.com/public/y_19971110.pdf.). Michael Hyatt reprinted Yardeni's testimony in his book *The Millennium Bug*, 233–40. It seems likely that Kennedy adapted this particular statement and then attributed it to Gates. Yardeni, apparently, was interpreting a 1997 Microsoft website statement (no longer available) which stated, "A single technology provider, even one as well prepared for the year 2000 as Microsoft, cannot solve all issues related to the transition to the year 2000" (as quoted by Yardeni, at www.yardeni.com/y2kbook.html). This 1997 Microsoft statement hardly expresses the despairing sentiment that Kennedy attributes to Gates. Furthermore, Don Jones, director of Year 2000 Readiness for Microsoft, confirmed our reading of Gates (E-mail from Angie Maddox, Y2K public relations representative, 3 August 1999).

24. Falwell, "Y2K Computer Crisis" (Part II).
25. Steve Hewitt, "Year 2000 Bug," Part I, *Christian Computing* Magazine (September 1998), from website at www.gospelcom.net/ccmag/y2k/sepy2k.html.
26. "Gates: Y2K fears overdone," CNNfn, 1 February 1999, retrieved from website at www.cnnfn.com/digitaljam/9902/01/davos_gates/.
27. Steve Hewitt, unpublished paper, April 1999. See "Survey of Professional Forecasters, Fourth Quarter 1998," Federal Reserve Bank of Philadelphia, 20 November 1998, at www.phil.frb.org/econ/spf/survq498.html; Robert A. Rankin, "Dealing with Y2K threat helps companies become more efficient," Knight Ridder Newspapers, 11 July 1999. Cf. "Survey of Professional Forecasters, Second Quarter, 1999," Federal Reserve Bank of Philadelphia, 21 May 1999, at www.phil.frb.org/econ/spf/survq299.html.

Chapter 7: Seven Frequently Asked Y2K Questions

1. See President's Council on Year 2000 Conversion website at www.y2k.gov/text/whatsnew1.html (retrieved 18 July 1999).
2. FDA website at www.fda.gov/cdrh/yr2000/yr2000.html (retrieved 21 July 1999).

3. "Telco Year 2000 Forum Expects No Major Disruption of Telephone Calls on January 1, 2000," *FCC News*, 3 March 1999, retrieved 21 July 1999 from the FCC website at www.fcc.gov/Bureaus/Miscellaneous/News_Releases/1999/nrmc9010.html.

4. "Statement of John A. Koskinen," 21 May 1999, retrieved 21 July 1999 from the U.S. Department of Agriculture's website at www.usda.gov/aphis/FSWG/roundtable.html. Koskinen is Assistant to the President and Chair, President's Council on Year 2000 Conversion.

5. Kennedy, "Y2K AND YOU," 4–5.

6. "Gates: Preparing for the Year 2000," 22 April 1998.

7. Sanders, "The Great Collapse," 9.

8. Lou Marcoccio, "Year 2000 International State of Readiness," U.S. Senate Testimony, 5 March 1999, from the Gartner Group website at http://gartner12.gartnerweb.com/public/static/y2k/y2k.html.

9. Falwell, Part I.

10. Special Report: Y2K Survival Guide, "Is It Safe to Fly? Will My ATM Work?" *Los Angeles Times*, Orange County edition, 21 June 1999, C8.

11. Ibid.

12. "Boeing and the Year 2000: Status Report," April 1999, emphasis added, from the Boeing website at www.boeing.com/companyoffices/aboutus/y2k/pmo/y2kbackgrounder.html.

13. "Is It Safe to Fly?" *Los Angeles Times*, C8.

14. "Frequently Asked Questions and Answers," from the United Airlines website at www.ual.com.

15. Jerry Greenwald, A Letter from the Chairman: "Safety in the Next Century," from the United Airlines website at www.ual.com.

16. Jack and Rexella Van Impe, *2000 Time Bomb* (Jack Van Impe Ministries), videotape. Cf. Dave Hunt, *Y2K: A Reasoned Response to Mass Hysteria* (Eugene, Ore.: Harvest House Publishers, 1999), 112, 174–5.

17. Hunt, 174–5.

18. John F. Walvoord and Roy B. Zuck, eds., *The Bible Knowledge Commentary: An Exposition of the Scriptures by Dallas Seminary Faculty* Old Testament (Victor Books, 1985), 1115. Cf. C.F. Keil and F. Delitzsch, *Commentary on the Old Testament*, Vol. VII (Grand Rapids, Mich.: William B. Eerdmans Publishing Co., 1976), 415–6.

19. "Is It Safe to Fly?" *Los Angeles Times*, C8.

20. Kennedy, "Y2K: WHAT CAN WE DO?" 14.

21. Associated Press, "Greenspan: Robbers Pose Y2K Threat," 6 May 1999.

22. Ibid. Regarding media hype Greenspan specifically said, "I know the evening news is going to play it as though we are looking at an asteroid which is about to hit us. . . . I am sure that people will get wise very soon and recognize that the last thing you want to do is draw inordinate amounts of currency out of the banks" (Ibid.). In addition, said Greenspan, "I'm increasingly less concerned about whether there will be true systemic problems" ("Greenspan Sees Only Modest Y2K Impact on Markets," *Reuters*, 6 May 1999 at www.y2k.govt.nz/news/reuters/120599/18.htm).

23. "Is It Safe to Fly?" *Los Angeles Times*, C8.

24. Jeffrey, *The Millennium Meltdown* (1998), 10.

25. "Journalists cautioned on Y2K reporting," *USA Today*, 10 March 1999, retrieved from www.usatoday.com/life/cyber/tech/cte613.htm.

26. *Focus on the Family* broadcast, 21 May 1999.

27. Bank of America website at www.bofa.com/y2k/index.cfm?section=7.

Epilogue

1. While Missler refers to Gary North as "an extremist" (Missler and Ankerberg, *Will American Survive the Y2K Crisis?*), Hyatt acknowledges his great indebtedness to Gary North: "Finally, Gary North, whose Web site literally made this book possible. He collected hundreds, if not thousands, of articles related to the Year 2000 Problem, which made my own research immeasurably easier. If by some miracle the problem is fixed in time and we somehow manage to avoid the meltdown of our society, it will be due in large part to the foresight of this watchman who sounded the trumpet when others were silent and spread the word on the Internet" (*The Millennium Bug*, 274–5).

2. As quoted in John Blanchard, *Gathered Gold* (Durham, N.C.: Evangelical Press, 1984), 83.

3. Piper, "Meditate on the Word of the Lord Day and Night."

Appendix

1. "Is It Safe to Fly?" *Los Angeles Times*, C1.

2. From "Disaster Supplies Kit," developed by the FEMA and the ARC, website at www.redcross.org/disaster/safety/supplies.html. See also www.redcross.org/disaster/safety/Y2K.html.

Select Bibliography

Articles

"15-year-old Boy Arrested for having Arsenal for Y2K," *Yahoo! News*, http://headlines.yahoo.com/Full_Coverage/Tech/Year_2000_Problem/, 28 April 1999.

Abrams, Jim. *Yahoo! News*, "CIA Sees Y2K Problems Overseas," dailynews.yahoo.com/headlines/ap/ap_headlines/story.html?s=v/ap/19990224/ts/y2k_problem_1.html, 24 February 1999.

American Red Cross. "Disaster Services—Disaster Supplies Kit," www.redcross.org/disaster/safety/supplies.html.

———. "Y2K: What You Should Know," www.redcross.org/disaster/safety/Y2K.html.

Anite Logical. "Auckland Power Failure—Anite's Swift Response," www.anite.com.au/Corp/PowerFailure.htm, 23 February 1999.

Ankerberg, John. "What Is 'the Y2K Problem' and How Should Christians Prepare?" www.ankerberg.com/anky2k.html, retrieved 23 February 1999.

Avalos, George. "Headaches Perhaps Biggest Danger in Flying on Jan. 1," *The Dallas Morning News*, 23 February 1999.

Bank of America. "Year 2000 FAQs," www.bankofamerica.com/y2k/index.cfm?section=7, 20 July 1999.

"Banks to Have Y2K Backup Plan," *USA Today*, www.usatoday.com/life/cyber/tech/ctf320.htm, 3 June 1999.

Bennett, Senator Bob. "Bennett Introduces Y2K Bill to Protect Americans' Pension Investments, Prevent Interruption of Many Essential Services," www.senate.gov/bennett/pr050598.html, 5 May 1998.

———. "Countdown to the Year 2000," www.senate.gov/bennett/cry2k.html, 11 May 1998.

———. "Hearing to Discuss Chances the Millennium Bug Will Cause the Nation's Power Grid to Fail," www.senate.gov/bennett/pr609b98.html, 9 June 1998.

"Bennett On Y2K: Warns of Civilization Breakdown," *Free Republic*, www.freerepublic.com, 16 July 1998.

"Boeing and the Year 2000: Status Report," www.boeing.com/company offices/aboutus/y2k/pmo/y2kbackgrounder.html, April 1999.

"Breaking the World's Food Chain: Agriculture and Y2K," CBN News, www.cbn.org/news/stories/981005.asp, 5 October 1998.

Buhler, Rich. "Scientists Discover Hell in Siberia," *Christianity Today*, 16 July 1990, 28.

Burkett, Larry. "Preparing for the 'Year 2000' Problem," *Money Matters*, published by Christian Financial Concepts, May 1998.

———. "Reality Hitting Home on Stocks, Taxes, and Y2K," *Money Matters*, published by Christian Financial Concepts, October 1998.

———. "Y2K: CFC's Position," *Christian Financial Concepts Y2K Position Paper*, www.cfcministry.org/library/Y2K/cfcY2Kposition.html, 27 May 1998.

———. "An Opportunity," *Money Matters*, published by Christian Financial Concepts, March 1999.

———. "Y2K: a 'Real and Serious' Threat," *Money Matters*, published by Christian Financial Concepts, June 1998.

———. "Awaiting the 'Churn' of the Century," *Money Matters*, published by Christian Financial Concepts, January 1998.

Caragata, Warren. "Guide to Y2K," *Maclean's*, 19 April 1999, 34.

Cerullo, Morris. "We Are Only 12 Months Away From Y2K Doom," http://www.mcwe.com/viewarticle.cgi?a=v&...ONTHS+AWAY+FROM+Y2K=DOOM&g=y&ident=geo, 15 April 1999.

Charlton, Angela. "Russia Admits Y2K Problem, Seeks Help From NATO and U.S.," *Orange County Register*, 4 February 1999.

Charski, Mindy. "The Golden Y2K Safety Net," *U.S. News & World Report*, 17 May 1999, 70

Chmielewski, Dawn C. "children Lured to porn on The Net," *Orange County Register*, 4 July 1999, 1.

"CIA Says Many Unprepared For Millennium Glitch," *CNN Interactive*, www.cnn.com/TECH/computing/9805/05/cia_2000.reut/, 5 May 1998.

CNNfn Financial Network, www.cnnfn.com/digitaljam/wires/9903/10/kelley_wg/, 10 March 1999.

CNNfn Financial Network. "Gates: Y2K Fears Overdone," cnnfn.com/digitaljam/9902/01/davos_gates/, 1 February 1999.

Core, E. L. "Don't Chase the Y2K Red Herrings," 13 April 1999, www.michaelhyatt.com/editorials/herrings.htm.

"Countdown to Chaos: Preparing for 2000," CBN News, www.cbn.org/news/stories/980323.asp, 23 March 1998.

Davidson, Dick. "Dick Davidson's Presentation to Cheyenne Rotary Club," Union Pacific Railroad, www.uprr.com/uprr/notes/corpcomm/3126.shtml, 2 December 1998.

De Borchgrave, Arnaud. " 'Millennium Bug' Battle a Case of Too Little, Too Late," *The Washington Times*, www.washtimes.com/news/news3.html, 2 April 1998.

DeMar, Gary. "An Antidote to Apocalypticism," *Biblical Worldview*, March 1999, 3.

De Jager, Peter. "Y2K: So Many Bugs . . . So Little Time," *Scientific American*, www.sciam.com/1999/0199issue/0199dejager.html.

"Dr. Falwell Updates Y2K Stance," *Christian Computing Magazine*, 21 May 1999.

Dunn, Ashley. "Home Largely Immune to Millennium Bug," *Los Angeles Times*, www.latimes.com/HOME/BUSINESS/UPDATES/lat_y2k990218.htm, 18 February 1999.

Dunn, Ashley. "Y2K Bug Poses Biggest Threat Outside the U.S.," *Los Angeles Times*, 6 June 1999.

Entous, Adam. "U.S. Agency Tells Americans Not to Panic Over Y2K," *Excite News*, http://nt.excite.com/news/r/990322/14/news-bug, 22 March 1999.

"Executive Orders and Laws Relating to National Emergencies Laws," www.disastercenter.com/laworder/laworder.htm, 1 March 1999.

"FAA At Risk: Y2K Impact on the Air Traffic Control System," Subcommittee on Technology, U.S. House of Representatives, www.house.gov/science/y2k_2–4.htm, 4 February 1998.

"Fed Plans Y2K Cash Reserve," ABC News, www.abcnews.com/sections/business/DailyNews/y2k_reserve980820/index.html, 20 August 1998.

Gates, Bill. "Preparing for The Year 2000," www.microsoft.com/BillGates/columns/1998essay/4–22colhtm, 22 April 1998.

Hartman, Greg. "Love Your Neighbor As Yourself: Year Two Thousand,"

Focus On The Family, July 1999, 10.

"Hawaiian Electric Company's Year 2000 Project," Hawaiian Electric Company, www.hei.com/heco/y2k/faq.htm, 19 February 1999.

Hewitt, Steve. "Year 2000 Bug: The Challenge Ahead," *Christian Computing Magazine*, September 1998.

"Horn Grades Federal Government on the Year 2000 Problem," House of Representatives Committee on Government Reform and Oversight News Release, 15 September 1997.

"Horn to Examine Year 2000 Computer Problem at FAA," House of Representatives Committee on Government Reform and Oversight New Release, 28 January 1998.

Hunt, Dave. "Y2K and Bible Prophecy." *The Berean Call*, Bend, Oregon, November 1998.

Hyatt, Michael. "A Christian Response to Y2K," *Ministries Today*, May/June 1999.

———. "A Personal Message About Y2K and Food From Michael Hyatt," www.michaelhyatt.com/food/message.htm, 6 May 1999.

———. "Frequently Asked Questions," www.michaelhyatt.com/faqs/faq1.htm, 24 February and 11 June 1999.

———. "Media Briefing—Examples," www.michaelhyatt.com/briefing/examples.htm, 20 April 1999.

———. "Statement of Michael S. Hyatt Before the Subcommittee on Government Management, Information and Technology," *Congress of the United States House of Representatives Committee on Government Reform and Oversight*, 24 September 1998.

———. "Y2K Editorial: Paul Revere Does 'About Face,' " at www.michaelhyatt.com/editorials/dejager.htm, 7 April 1999.

———. "Y2K Personal Survival Guide, Appendix A: An Overview of Y2K," at www.michaelhyatt.com/survival/xappendixa.htm.

"IRS 2000: A Time Bomb for Taxpayers," *CBN News*, www.cbn.org/news/stories/980330b.asp, 30 March 1998.

"Johnson Announces Hearing on the Year 2000 Computer Problem," Advisory From the Committee on Ways and Means," www.house.gov/htbin/fens-search/comms/wm . . . /aaa6NjNEa8e979d&NS-doc-offset?, 30 April 1998.

Johnson, Glenn. "FAA: Air Travel Safe Despite Y2K," *Yahoo! News*, www.dailynews.yahoo.com/headlines/tc/story.html?s=v/nm/19990305/tc/millennium_11.html, 5 March 1999.

Junod, Tom. "365 Days to the Apocalypse and We Still Don't Know Where to Hide the Jews . . . and other notes from Pat Robertson's Y2K conference," *Esquire*, January 1999.

Kellner, Mark A. "Y2K: A Secular Apocalypse?" *Christianity Today*, 11 January 1999.

Kennedy, Bruce. "Learning to Love Y2K," *CNN Interactive*, http://www.cnn.com/TECH/specials/y2k/stories/y2k.blessing/, 17 May 1999.

Kim, Jane J. "Citicorp, Chase to Spend Millions on Millennium Bug," *The Wall Street Journal*, 27 February 1998.

Kirsner, Scott. "Year 2000 Challenge—Interview with the Czar," *CIO Magazine*, www.cio.com/archive/080198_y2k_content.html, 1 August 1998.

Lacayo, Richard. "The End of the Word As We Know It?" *Time*, January 18, 1999, 60.

Lesher, Dave. "State Computers 75% Free of Y2K Problems," *Los Angeles Times*, www.latimes.com/HOME/NEWS/ASECTION/t000015169.html, 18 February 1999.

Levy, Steven and Katie Hafner. "The Millennium: The Day the World Shuts Down," *Newsweek*, 2 June 1997.

Levy, Steven. "Will the Bug Bite the Bull?" *Newsweek*, 4 May 1998.

Lindsay, Walter. "Swatting the Millennium Bug," www.chalcedon.edu/report/98feb/Lindsay_Millennium.html, 8 June 1998.

Marcoccio, Lou. "Year 2000 International State of Readiness," Gartner Group, 5 March 1999.

Marrs, Texe. "Days of Hunger, Days of Chaos," *Power of Prophecy*, Austin, TX: Power of Prophecy, February 1999.

McCullagh, Declan. "IRS Vs. Y2K," *Time Digital*, 8 March 1999.

McCullagh, Declan and Bruce Van Voorst. "Why the Government's Machines Won't Make It," *Time*, Vol. 151, No. 23, www.pathfinder.com/time/magazine/1998/dom/980615/technology_why_the_gover.html, 15 June 1998

McUsic, Teresa. "Technology Not Used Well, Gates Says," *Orange County Register*, 17 May 1999.

"Medicare 2000: Dead on Arrival?" *CBN News*, www.cbn.org/news/stories/980413.asp, 13 April 1998.

Mercury Energy. "Mercury Energy Submissions—CBD Power Failure Caused By Combination of Factors," www.mercury.co.nz/media/frame.asp?loc=edia_95.html, 21 May 1998.

Merx, Katie. "Y2K Showdown Arrives Early," *Detroit News*, www.detnews.com/1999/technology/9902/17/02170168.htm, 17 February 1999.

Microsoft TechNet. "Microsoft Year 2000 Readiness Disclosure and Resource

Center," www.microsoft.com/technet/year2k/2kfaq/related/2kpc/2kpc01.htm, 25 March 1999.

Mitchell, Chris. "Countdown to Chaos?" *Charisma*, December 1998.

"Mormon Policy vs. Mormons' Practice," Walton Feed, www.waltonfeed.com/self/north/mormon.htm, 25 March 1999.

Olenick, Doug. "Gates Addresses Y2K and the Future," *Computer Retail Week*, www.crw.com/news/1998/weekending120498/229news003.asp, 7 December 1998.

"Organizers Say Y2K to Blame for Demise of Minneapolis Millennium Party," *CNN Interactive*, www.cnn.com/US/9905/09/AM-Celebration-Canceled.ap/, 9 May 1999.

Parsley, David. "Microsoft: We Have Been Bitten by Millennium Bug," *Sunday Times*, www.Sunday-times.co.uk/news/pages/sti/98/11/29/stibusnws01015.html?1733620, 29 November 1998.

Piper, John. "Meditate On The Word of the Lord Day and Night," www.soundofgrace.com/piper99/1–3–99.htm, Bethlehem Baptist Church, 3 January 1999.

Pugliese, David. "'Martial Law' Rushed for Y2K Chaos," *The Ottawa Citizen*, 12 December 1998.

Ratcliffe, Mitch. "Y2K hits April 1: What to expect," MSNBC, www.msnbc.com/255009.asp, 1 April 1999.

Religion Today. "Y2K: How Should We Then Live?" www.religiontoday.com/Archive/FeatureStory/View.cgi?file=19980918.s1.html, *USA Today*, 18 September 1998.

"Remarks by the President Concerning the Year 2000 Conversion," The White House, Office of the Press Secretary, www.whitehouse.gov/WH/New/html/19980714–5571.html, 14 July 1998.

"Right Year, Wrong Century," *The LaCrosse Tribune*, LaCrosse, WI, 29 March 1993.

Sanko, John. "Will Prison Gates Fly Open in January 2000?" Inside Denver, *Denver Rocky Mountain News*, 11 June 1998.

"Serious Y2K Risks in Embedded Systems—Report," *South China Morning Post*, Technology Section, 26 April 1999.

Snow, Kate. "Y2K Could Affect Flow of U.S. Oil Imports," *CNN*, www.cnn.com/TECH/computing/9903/21/bigpicture.y2k.hln/, 21 March 1999.

"Survey of Professional Forecasters, Fourth Quarter, 1999," Federal Reserve Bank of Philadelphia, www.phil.frb.org/econ/spf/survq498.html, 20 November 1998.

"Survey of Professional Forecasters, First Quarter, 1999," Federal Reserve Bank of Philadelphia, www.phil.frb.org/econ/spf/survq199.html, 22 February 1999.

"Survey of Professional Forecasters, Second Quarter, 1999," Federal Reserve Bank of Philadelphia, www.phil.frb.org/econ/spf/survq299.html, 21 May 1999.

"Surviving the Crisis: How to Prepare for Y2K," CBN News, www.cbn.org/news/stories/980710.asp, 10 July 1998.

Taylor, Sean. "Debugging the Millennium Bug," *On Mission*, March-April 1999.

"The Golden Y2K Safety Net," *U.S. News & World Report*, 17 May 1999, 70.

"The Year 2000: A Date With Disaster," CBN News, www.cbn.org/news/stories/980602.asp, 2 June 1998.

"The Year 2000 Problem: Status Report on Federal, State, Local and Foreign Governments," Congress of the United States, House of Representatives Committee on Government Reform, 20 January 1999.

Underhill, Glynnis. "SA Reserve Bank Stockpiles Cash In Case of Y2K Panic," *AfricaNews*, www.africanews.org/south/southafrica/stories/19990215_feat20.html, 15 February 1999.

Van Eyck, Zack. "No Screeching Halt on Jan. 1," *Deseret News*, www.desnews.com/dn/view/0,1249,65000176,00.html?, 4 March 1999.

Watanabe, Teresa. "The Year of Believing Prophecies," *Los Angeles Times*, 31 March 1999.

Weil, Nancy. "Global Y2K: The Great Unknown," CNNiN Interactive, www.cnn.com/TECH/computing/9906/08/overseas.y2k.id, 8 June 1999.

"What Requires an Upgrade Because of the Year 2000?" Diebold Incorporated, http://www2.diebold.com/nasey2k/Y2K_Upgrades.htm, 10 May 1999.

Willenssen, Joel C. "Year 2000 Computing Crisis, Testimony of Joel C. Willenssen, Director, Civil Agencies Information Systems."

Yardeni, Ed. "Year 2000 Recession? Prepare For the Worst, Hope For the Best," www.yardeni.com/y2kbook.html, 14 February 1999.

"Year 2000 Computing Crisis: Readiness of the Electric Power Industry," Report to the Committee on the Year 2000 Technology Problem, U.S. Senate, April 1999.

"Y2K Blackout? Keeping the Power in America's Power Grid," CBN News, www.cbn.org/news/stories/980609.asp, 9 June 1998.

"Y2K Lawsuit Bill Passed by Congress," *USA Today*, www.usatoday.com/life/cybertech/ctf520.htm, 2 July 1999.

Audiotapes

Burkett, Larry. "Our Economy in Crisis," Oasis International Ltd., 1994.

Burkett, Larry and Chuck Missler. "Y2K: Facing the Challenge," National Religious Broadcasters, 2 February 1999.

DeMar, Gary and Gary North, Ralph Barker. "The Millennial Bug." 6 June 1997.

Dobson, James; "Y2K: Expectations and Preparations," 21–23 October 1998. Focus on the Family.

Falwell, Jerry. "The Y2K Computer Crisis," Parts I & II, Tapes 98:131 & 98:136.

Farrar, Steve. "God, Y2K, and You!" UPWORDS, San Antonio: 8 November 1998.

Feldhahn, Shaunti. "Y2K," First Edition, n.d.

Gause, Andrew. "Y2K and Martial Law," Point of View Radio Talk Show with Marlin Maddoux, Dallas: 25 June 1999.

Hunt, Dave and Gary Hedrick, Steve Hewitt. "The Truth About Y2K," *The Berean Call*, Bend, Oregon.

Hyatt, Michael. "Planning For Y2K," *Focus on the Family*, 11 & 12 January 1999.

———. "Y2K: What Every Christian Should Know," Nelson Audio Books on Cassette, March 1999. Two Tapes.

Kline, Ken. "Millennium Bug," Parts 1–4. Southwest Radio Church, 1998.

Lindsay, Walter and R. J. Rushdoony. "The Millennium Computer Bug," December 1997.

Michaels, John. "Bringing Balance to Y2K." Calvary Chapel Costa Mesa, 28 January 1999.

Missler, Chuck and Ed Yourdon, Jim Lord, Tom Cloud. "Y2K: Your Questions Answered by the Experts," Koinonia House, Coeur d'Alene, ID; 1999. Two Tapes.

Noriel, Les. "The Y2K Problem." Westminster Theological Seminary, February 1999.

North, Gary and Duncan Long. "Picking a Safe Place," n.d.

North, Gary. "The Millennium Manifesto," n.d.

Booklets

Kennedy, D. James. *Y2K and You*. Fort Lauderdale: Coral Ridge Ministries, 1999.

———. *Y2K: What Can We Do?* Fort Lauderdale: Coral Ridge Ministries, 1999.

North, Gary. *Building Untouchable Wealth*, Remnant Review, Baltimore: Agora, Inc., 1997.

———. *Built On a Lie: The Surprising Truth About Banks*, Remnant Review, Baltimore: Agora, Inc., 1997.

Shilling, Gary L. *Y2K Planning For Survival*, Warrenton, VA. 15 March 1999.

Books

Abanes, Richard. *End-Time Visions: The Road to Armageddon?* Nashville: Broadman & Holman Publishers, 1998.

Bennett, Senator Robert F. and Senator Christopher J. Dodd. *The Senate Special Report on Y2K*. Nashville: Thomas Nelson Publishers, 1999.

Bickel, Bruce and Stan Jantz. *Bruce & Stan's Guide to the End of the World*. Eugene, Ore.: Harvest House Publishers, 1999.

Burkett, Larry. *The Coming Economic Earthquake*. Chicago: Moody Press, 1991.

Christopher, David N. *The Y2K Urban Survival Guide For The Father / Husband / Mother / Wife / Provider / Protector*. Ventura, Calif.: Self-published, 1998.

Coral Ridge Ministries. *Answers To The Most Important Questions About Y2K*, Fort Lauderdale: Coral Ridge Ministries, 1998.

Cummings, Judith. *Plan A: An Optimist Prepares for Y2K*, Boys Town, Nebr.: Rehoboth Publishing, 1998.

De Jager, Peter and Richard Bergeon. *Managing 00: Surviving the Year 2000 Computing Crisis*. New York: Wiley Computer Publishing, 1997.

DeMar, Gary. *Last Days Madness*, Atlanta: American Vision, Inc., 1997.

Farrar, Steve. *Spiritual Survival During the Y2K Crisis*. Nashville: Thomas Nelson Publishers, 1999.

Feldhahn, Shaunti Christine. *Y2K: The Millennium Bug*. Sisters, Ore.: Multnomah Publishers, 1998.

———. *Y2K: The Millennium Bug Resource Guide*. Sisters, Ore.: Multnomah Publishers, 1998.

Ford, Cliff. *Blood, Money, & Greed: The Money Trust Conspiracy*. Beverly Hills: Western Front Ltd., 1998.

Froese, Arno and Joel Froese. *When Y2K Dies*. Columbia, S.C.: The Olive Press, a division of Midnight Call Ministries, 1999.

Guinness, Os. *Fit Bodies, Fat Minds*, Grand Rapids, Mich.: Baker Books, 1994.

Hunt, Dave. *Y2K: A Reasoned Response to Mass Hysteria*. Eugene, Ore.: Harvest House Publishers, 1999.

Hutchings, Noah, Larry Spargimno and David Hutchins. *Y2K=666*. Oklahoma City: Hearthstone Publishing, 1998.

Hyatt, Michael and George Grant. *Y2K: The Day The World Shut Down*. Nashville: Word Publishing, 1998.

Hyatt, Michael S. *The Millennium Bug: How to Survive the Coming Chaos*. Washington, D.C.: Regnery Publishing, Inc., 1998.

———. *The Y2K Personal Survival Guide*. Washington, D.C.: Regnery Publishing, Inc., 1999.

Jeffrey, Grant R. and Angela Hunt. *Flee The Darkness*. Nashville: Word Publishing, 1998.

Jeffrey, Grant R. *The Millennium Meltdown*. Toronto: Frontier Research Publications, 1998.

Lindsey, Hal and Cliff Ford. *Facing Millennial Midnight*. Beverly Hills: Western Front Ltd., 1998.

Paris, James L. *The Christian Financial Crisis*. Daytona Beach, Fla.: Avatar Publishing Group, Inc., 1999.

MacGregor, Jerry and Kirk Charles. *Y2K Family Survival Guide*. Eugene, Ore.: Harvest House Publishers, 1999.

McAlvany, Donald S. *The Y2K Tidal Wave*. Toronto: Frontier Research Publications, Inc., 1999.

Missler, Chuck and Mark Eastman. *Alien Encounters*. Coeur d'Alene, Idaho: Koinonia House, 1997.

Yardeni, Ed. *Year 2000 Recession? Net Book*, Version 10.0, 15 February 1999.

———. *Year 2000 Recession? Net Book*, Version 11.0, 7 March 1999.

Yourdon, Edward and Jennifer Yourdon. *Time Bomb 2000*. Upper Saddle River, N.J.: Prentice Hall PTR, 1998.

Magazines

Personal Update, Koinonia House.

Tabletalk, Lake Mary, Fla.: Ligonier Ministries, April 1999.

Time magazine, January 18, 1999. Multiple articles.

World Magazine, April 3, 1999. "Y2K: Prudent Preparation or January Fool's Day?"

Newsletters

Christian Reconstruction, Gary North, various issues.
Dominion Strategies, Gary North, various issues.
Gary North's Remnant Review, Gary North, various issues.
Institute for Christian Economics, Gary North, various issues.

Pamphlets

"The Crisis and Confusion of Y2K," CBN News Special Report, Virginia Beach, VA: Christian Broadcasting Network Inc., 1998.
"The Millennium Bug and The Year Two Thousand," Kenn Kline, Southwest Radio Church, n.d.

Transcripts

Kroft, Steve. "Y2K: Look at How Local Governments, Including Washington, DC, Are Less Prepared For a Possible Y2K Crash Than Many Think," *60 Minutes* Transcript, 23 May 1999.
"The Y2K Problem," Senator Robert Bennett, Senator Christopher Dodd, Ed Yardeni, Morris Dees on *Face The Nation*, 28 February 1999.

Videotapes

Bennett, Robert, Gordon Smith, Christopher Dodd. Y2K News Conference, C-Span, 2 March 1999.
"Countdown to Y2K: The Coming Storm," Grant Jeffrey, James Stevens, Ed Yourdon. Inspirational Network, 1998.
Falwell, Jerry. "Y2K: A Christian's Survival Guide," Thomas Road Baptist Church, 30 August 1998.
Hewitt, Steve. "The Challenge Ahead," *Christian Computing Magazine*, 3 March 1999.
Jeffrey, Grant. "The Millennium Meltdown—Year 2000," 1998.
Kennedy, D. James. "Y2K: No Turning Back," *Coral Ridge Hour*, Santa Ana, CA: Trinity Broadcasting Network, 31 January 1999.
Klein, Ken. "Millennium Bug and The Year 2000," Ken Klein Ministries, 1997.
Lindsey, Hal and Cliff Ford. "Facing Millennial Midnight," 1999.
Marrs, Texe. "Y2K: Hidden Dangers of Martial Law and a Police State,"

RiverCrest Publishing: Austin, TX. 1999.

Missler, Chuck and John Ankerberg. "Will America Survive the Y2K Crisis?" Coeur d'Alene, Idaho: Koinonia House, 1998.

Robertson, Pat. "Y2K and the Church," *700 Club*, Christian Broadcasting Network, 1998.

Smith, Craig. "Millennium Fears." PAX TV, 18 April 1999.

———. *Praise the Lord*, Trinity Broadcasting Network, 17 March 1998.

Van Impe, Jack and Rexella Van Impe. *2000 Time Bomb*, Jack Van Impe Ministries, 1998.

Websites

Advanced System Technologies Ltd.—Y2K Links
http://astuk.com/links.htm

American Red Cross
http://www.redcross.org/disaster/safety/y2k.html

Answers in Action
http://www.answers.org

CIO Magazine—15 September 1996: Year 2000 Online Resources
http://www.cio.com/forums/091596_2kresources.html882298308

Disaster Center
http://www.disastercenter.com

Dr. Ed Yardeni's Economics Network
http://www.yardeni.com/887134808

EDS Vendor 2000
http://www.vendor2000.com

Ed Yourdon's Home Page
http://yourdon.com

Federal Emergency Management Agency Y2K Issues
http://www.fema.gov/y2k

FEMA's Y2K for Kids
http://www.fema.gov/kids/y2k.htm

FEMA's Preparedness Recommendations
http://www.fema.gov/pte/prepare.htm

GartnerGroup Interactive
http://gartner5.gartnerweb.com/public/static/home/home.html

Gary North's Y2K Links and Forums—Newest Links
http://garynorth.com/y2k/latest_.cfm

Harlan Smith—Y2K Report

http://www.scotsystems.com/hsmithy2k.html882287544

IBM Canada Year 2000 solutions
http://www.can.ibm.com/year2000/882295036

Koinonia House
http://www.khouse.org

Michael S. Hyatt's Y2Kprep
http://www.michaelhyatt.com

Microsoft Consumer Year 2000 Resources
http://computingcentral.com/guide/year2000/MSY2k

Microsoft TechNet—Year 2000
http://www.microsoft.com/technet/year2k

Microsoft Year 2000 Resource Center
http://www.microsoft.com/y2k

Mitre/Esc Year 2000
http://www.mitre.org/technology/y2k

NSTL Ymark2000
http://www.nstl.com/html/nstl_ymark2000.html

Personal Y2K Supplies
http://www.mindspring.com/tedderryberry/Y2Ksupplies.htm

Prepare4Y2K
http://www.prepare4y2k.com

President's Council on Year 2000 Conversion
http://www.y2k.gov

Securities and Exchange Commission
http://www.sec.gov/news/home2000.htm

Small Business Administration
http://www.sba.gov/y2k

Special Committee on the Year 2000 Technology Problem
http://www.senate.gov/y2k/home.html

Subcommittee on Government Management, Information and Technology
http://www.house.gov/reform/gmit/index.htm

Symantec Free BIOS Test and Fix
http://www.symantec.com/sabu/n2000/fs_retail.html

The Millennium Bug
http://www.year2000.co.uk/year2000.htm887989318

Unisys Year 2000 Home Page
http://www.marketplace.unisys.com/year2000/882295896

United Airlines Company Information
http://www.ual.com/airline/default.asp?section‚ear_

2000.asp&SubCategoryØur_Company&destination_URL/airline/Our_
Company/Year_2000.asp
University of Illinois at Urbana-Champaign Year 2000 Computing Issues
http://y2k.cso.uiuc.edu/
U.S. Government Accounting Office
http://www.gao.gov/y2kr.htm
Westergaard Year 2000
http://www.y2ktimebomb.com/884638081
WorldNetDaily—A Free Press for a Free People
http://www.worldnetdaily.com
Yahoo! Full Coverage—Year 2000 Problem
http://headlines.yahoo.com/Full_Coverage/Tech/Year_2000_Problem
Year 2000 Conversion
http://www.y2k.gov/java/contingency.html
Year 2000 glitch repairs behind—12/19/97
http://detnews.com/1998/cyberia/9801/12/12190083.htm
Year 2000 Information Center—Archive of Articles and Other Items
http://www.year2000.com/y2karchive.html882218812
Year 2000 Information Center—Year 2000 Press Clippings
http://www.year2000.com/y2karticles.html
Year 2000 Journal
http://www.y2kjournal.com/884633326
Y2K—Frequently Asked Questions
http://www.itpolicy.gsa.gov/mks/yr2000/faq.htm
Y2K Manuscript
http://www.calvarychapel.org/springvalley/y2k1.htm
Y2K News Magazine
http://www.y2knews.com/902418333
Y2K Resource Center on Year 2000 Computer Problems, Millennium Bug in
Y2K CBN News
http://www.cbn.org/y2k/index.asp
Y2K—The Year 2000
http://ntg-inter.com/ntg/y2k/info/y2kinfo.htm882294619

Scripture Index

Subject Index

About the Author

HANK HANEGRAAFF answers questions live as host of the *Bible Answer Man* broadcast, heard daily throughout the United States and Canada. He is president of the world-renowned Christian Research Institute headquartered in Southern California and author of the bestselling Gold Medallion winner *Christianity in Crisis* as well as the award-winning bestsellers *Counterfeit Revival* and *The Face*.

As author of Memory Dynamics, Hank has developed memorable tools to prepare believers to effectively communicate (1) *what* they believe, (2) *why* they believe it, and (3) *where* cults deviate from Christianity. He has also developed fun and easy techniques for memorizing Scripture quickly and retaining it forever.

Hank is a popular speaker for churches and conferences worldwide. He resides in Southern California with his wife, Kathy, and their eight children: Michelle, Katie, David, John Mark, Hank Jr., Christina, Paul, and Faith.

For further information on Memory Dynamics and Personal Witness Training materials, address your request to:

Hank Hanegraaff
Box 80250
Rancho Santa Margarita, CA 92688–0250
or call (949) 589–1504

The Millennium Bug Debugged Available on Tape

For a dynamic audiotape version of *The Millennium Bug Debugged* by Hank Hanegraaff, contact the Christian Research Institute, PO Box 7000, Rancho Santa Margarita, CA 92688; phone: (949) 858-6100; fax (949) 858-6111; or log on to www.equip.org.